D0843225

WITHDRAWN

Literary Criticism in Perspective
Kafka's Castle and the Critical Imagination

*Studies in German Literature, Linguistics,
and Culture*

James Hardin & Gunther Holst
Managing Editors

Editorial Board
Literary Criticism in Perspective

James Hardin (*South Carolina*), General Editor

Eitel Timm (*Waldorf School, Vancouver*), German Literature

Benjamin Franklin V (*South Carolina*), American and
English Literature

Reingard M. Nischik (*Constance*), Comparative Literature

About *Literary Criticism in Perspective*

Books in the series *Literary Criticism in Perspective*, a subseries of *Studies in German Literature, Linguistics, and Culture,* and *Studies in English and American Literature, Linguistics, and Culture,* trace literary scholarship and criticism on major and neglected writers alike, or on a single major work, a group of writers, a literary school or movement. In so doing the authors — authorities on the topic in question who are also well-versed in the principles and history of literary criticism — address a readership consisting of scholars, students of literature at the graduate and undergraduate level, and the general reader. One of the primary purposes of the series is to illuminate the nature of literary criticism itself, to gauge the influence of social and historic currents on aesthetic judgments once thought objective and normative.

Kafka's Castle and the Critical Imagination

Stephen D. Dowden

Kafka's Castle
and the
Critical Imagination

C A M D E N H O U S E

Published by Camden House, Inc.
Drawer 2025
Columbia, SC 29202 USA

Printed on acid-free paper.
Binding materials are chosen for strength and
durability.

ISBN: 1-57113-004-7

Library of Congress Cataloging-in Publication Data

Dowden, Stephen D.
 Kafka's castle and the critical imagination / Stephen D. Dowden.
  p.   cm. -- (Studies in German literature, linguistics, and
culture) (Literary criticism in perspective)
 Includes bibliographical references and index.
 ISBN 1-57113-004-7 (alk. paper)
 1. Kafka, Franz, 1883-1924. Schloss. I. Title. II. Series.
III. Series: Studies in German literature, linguistics, and culture
(Unnumbered)
PT2621.A26S3975   1995
833'. 912--dc20   94-46933
                                                    CIP

"I sometimes wonder if *The Castle* isn't in fact linked to Kafka's own erotic blockage — a book engaged at every level with not reaching a climax."

He laughs at my speculation, but as before, gently and with that unrelenting amiability. Yes, just so profoundly compromised is the retired professor, caught, as in a mangle, between conscience and the regime — between conscience and searing abdominal pain. "Well," he says, putting a hand on my arm in a kind and fatherly way, "to each obstructed citizen his own Kafka."

"And to each angry man his own Melville," I reply. "But then what are bookish people to do with all the great prose they read — "

"— but sink their teeth into it. Exactly. Into the books, instead of the hand that throttles them."

— *The Professor of Desire*, by Philip Roth

Contents

Acknowledgments

Ingeborg C. Henel, my friend and my mentor in Kafka studies, never wrote much about *Das Schloß*. When I asked her why, she frankly told me the reason for her silence was that she found Kafka's last novel baffling. Eventually she and I read the book together in a series of sittings at her apartment in Hamden, Connecticut. I have profited immensely from the uncompromising hard-headedness with which she listens to and probes Kafka's text. By the time we finished our study of the novel, neither of us had the feeling that we had come to grips with it. I took up this project as my continuation of our efforts, and this book is gratefully dedicated to her.

I also owe a debt of gratitude to other friends who have in various ways contributed to and challenged my thinking about Kafka: Willi Goetschel, Joe Lawrence, Pamela Rothstein (my wife), Howard Stern (the Magus of Middletown), and especially David Suchoff, whose Kafka essays and conversations have lastingly influenced my imagination.

S. D. D.
September 1994

Translations

Throughout the text I have quoted Kafka first in German and then in English. Even though translations of Kafka are readily available, they do not yet follow the critical edition of his complete writings, which began appearing in the early eighties. Rather than separating the accurate translations from the infelicitous ones, those affected by the critical edition from those not, I have elected for the sake of both accuracy and simplicity to make my own. With few exceptions, French and German literary criticism is cited in English only and from published translations where available. When a passage in English is referred to a text in French or German with no translation listed next to it the bibliography, the translation is my own. The reference date will always be to the original date of publication. For example, the entry (Robert 1963:123) gives the date of the French publication of Marthe Robert's *L'ancien et le nouveau*, while my page reference is to Carol Cosman's later translation of it, which is listed in my bibliography with the original.

Abbreviations

Works by Franz Kafka

B   *Briefe 1902–1924.* Ed. Max Brod. New York: Schocken, 1958.

MBFK   *Max Brod Franz Kafka, Eine Freundschaft. Briefwechsel.* Ed. Malcolm Pasley. 2 vols. Frankfurt am Main: S. Fischer, 1989.

NS2   *Nachgelassene Schriften und Fragmente II.* Ed. Jost Schillemeit. Frankfurt am Main: S. Fischer, 1992.

P   *Der Proceß. Roman in der Fassung der Handschrift.* Ed. Malcolm Pasley. Frankfurt am Main: S. Fischer, 1990.

S   *Das Schloß. Roman in der Fassung der Handschrift.* Ed. Malcolm Pasley. Frankfurt am Main: S. Fischer, 1982.

Sa   *Das Schloß. Kommentarband.* Ed. Malcolm Pasley. Frankfurt am Main: S. Fischer, 1982.

T   *Tagebücher in der Fassung der Handschrift.* Eds. Hans-Gerd Koch, Michael Müller, Malcolm Pasley. Frankfurt am Main: S. Fischer, 1990.

1: Introduction

HEINZ POLITZER, ONE of the preeminent Kafka critics, famously wrote that Kafka's works are like a Rorschach test. They reveal not Kafka's meaning but the thoughts and predispositions of the critic. He was right, of course, and reader response criticism has since raised such observations to a high degree of formal specificity. This is true not just for Kafka — though his strangely accommodating fiction remains a conspicuously busy site of readerly participation in the production of meaning — but for literature as a whole.

Still, anyone who has read a lot of Kafka criticism is likely to come to a view opposite Politzer's. By comparison with the secondary literature it has produced, Kafka's fiction is exemplary in its single-minded clarity. Instead, it is the criticism that looks like a vast and shapeless Rorschach blotch. It isn't, of course, but its massive size and diversity are not easily managed. It would seem that Kafka criticism has assimilated the structure of the problem whose opacity occasioned its genesis in the first place.

The present book is an attempt to discern shape and pattern in the pieces of the blotch that concern themselves with Kafka's novel *Das Schloß*. The effort is predicated on the assumption that one good way to understand *Das Schloß* is to come to terms with the place Kafka and his baffling novels have come to hold in the critical imagination. At this late date in Kafka studies it has become clear that *Das Schloß* is not likely to give up its deepest secrets, if indeed it has any. The narrative may well be pure surface. Either way, its place in twentieth-century fiction remains assured. Therefore it would be well to understand exactly how and for what reasons critics have imagined its meaning. It will be the task of the pages that follow to chart the course of Kafka's unfinished novel manuscript from his desk drawer to its stable, yet constantly changing, status as a modernist classic.

My desire to write such a book has developed from the Kafka seminars I have taught over the last decade or so. In these classes it has been my practice to assign readings from the standard works of Kafka criticism, which has its own well-established interior canon, to clarify the diversity of critical standpoints that have gone into the construction of Kafka the classic modernist. The students, graduates and undergraduates alike, have found the Babylonian confusion of Kafka criticism almost as bewildering as Kafka's fiction. I believe the source of the puzzlement is not that the individual works themselves are more recondite than most, but that it is difficult to relate these works of criticism to each other.

The problem has to do with Politzer's Rorschach effect. Since it seems possible to make almost any kind of case about Kafka stick — from astrological to psychobiographical to deconstructive, from Marxism to Jewish mysticism — the word *Kafka* stands for a playing field in the great free-for-all of literary critical method. Not extraordinary in itself, this situation simply reflects the larger, lively complexities of contemporary literary study. Still, Kafka criticism may well experience the conflict of voices more intensely than most other writer-focused venues. The large volume of literature and the clash of opinions within Kafka criticism obscure the view of Kafka when they are taken too seriously. This is not news. Kafka scholars have been grousing about the bulky corpus of secondary literature since the early fifties. What should attract our thoughtful attention instead are the specific reasons for the confusion: the underlying grid of historical contingencies, critical predispositions, ideologically or unconsciously motivated prejudices, and theoretical assumptions but also the inadvertencies and sheer acts of imagination that have bestowed upon *Das Schloß* its received meanings.

There can be no permanently true or correct reading of *Das Schloß* because Kafka's powerful imagination simultaneously accommodates, resists, and exceeds every available method of interpretation. This holds good to some degree for any strong literary text. But it is especially true of *Das Schloß* because of its unique combination of parable-like simplicity and unyielding opacity. And as if this were not in itself difficult enough, the available forms of interpretation keep shifting, from historical moment to historical moment, from individual to individual, and from theory to theory. There is no escape from contingency. Therefore, the assumptions that guide my efforts in the present book are not and cannot be neutral. Just as there is no archimedean point from which to lift *Das Schloß* out of the hinges on which it turns, so is there none from which to judge the criticism. Art can be autonomous, but historical surveys of criticism cannot. Therefore I must declare my own critical standpoint.

Cultural critique is the perspective that has most shaped my view of *Das Schloß* and its reception. I have attempted in what follows to elucidate the criticism against the historical and cultural background in which it took shape. Chapter one discusses the precanonical Kafka against the background of Weimar Germany's intellectual life. Kafka, though a citizen of the new Czech Republic and culturally an Austrian, was writing in German mainly for a small German audience. Chapter two explores his rise to canonical status in the era of the Cold War. Chapter three explores the formalist turn of Kafka criticism after the failure of the 1968 student revolt (to accept a somewhat arbitrary turning point), and chapter four examines the attempt of literary critics to look more closely at the meaning of context and history in an attempt to correct the perceived excesses of poststructuralist formalism. It is the moment of cultural criticism that defines my approach, for the most part, though in the last chapter I develop my own view of the novel in such a way as to illuminate a blind spot within cultural criticism.

The practitioners of cultural critique generally take a dim view of ontology and autonomy in literature because claims to ahistorical and noncontingent value seem politically suspect to them. There are good historical reasons for this. The claim to have discovered some universal human trait or value usually turns out to be a strategy for asserting the superiority of whatever happen to be one's own historical, contingent preferences. As many critics have noted in the past, Kafka was predisposed in the direction of universals. In his writing he hoped to lift the world into the true, timeless, and immutable as he put it in a famous passage of 1917 from his diary. In my final chapter I will try to clarify the specific meaning of such claims and then try to show what bearing this ought to have on our understanding of *Das Schloß*, and I will argue that it should not worry the contemporary advocates of liberal cultural critique.

If it at first seems odd to conclude a critical survey of secondary literature with an essay of my own, it should on second thought seem not only reasonable but obligatory. With the benefit of hindsight it is all too easy to find fault with people who have written about a work as obdurately protean as *Das Schloß*, and I have sometimes been blunt in my demurrals. It is only fair that I too should take the risk of saying something sensible about Kafka's most baffling imaginative achievement.

The first chapter sets the stage. Kafka died of tuberculosis in 1924, a time perceived by German intellectuals of the right and left, from Heidegger and Jaspers to Benjamin and Adorno, as one of deep spiritual crisis. Kafka's fiction belongs to this era. His novels and other unpublished works began to appear shortly after his death under the editorship of Max Brod, who diligently promoted the reputation of his late friend but also worked hard to establish as true his own image of Kafka as a saintly writer principally concerned with religious matters. At first this view was largely accepted, with only a few important voices of opposition, notably Siegfried Kracauer, Walter Benjamin, Hannah Arendt, and Günther Anders.

The war interrupted the reception of Kafka's works, of course, but it also paved the way for the postwar reception. The Holocaust conditioned his reception in obvious ways, but what the second chapter focuses most attention on is how cultural politics during the Cold War helped to establish and shape Kafka's reputation. While Kafka was partly understood as a voice representing the last generation of intellectual Western European Jewry, and therefore an unimpeachable witness against the bestiality of Nazism, at the same time he rose meteorically into the politically dubious company of high literary modernism. There he joined a company of literary titans whose ethics and politics more often than not inclined them toward a sympathy, sometimes latent and sometimes not, with totalitarian practices.

Moreover, the political configuration of the Cold War added yet another dimension to the Kafka problem. Like the other modernists, Kafka was perceived to be a subversive imagination. His advocates, Walter Jens and Wilhelm Emrich, for example, perceived him as subversive of totalitarianism of any sort and attempted to harness his prestige on behalf of a postwar liberalism. Lionel Trilling, however, found himself ill at ease with Kafka's political implications, fearing that the subversive aspects of Kafka's achievement ran too deep to be contained by well-meaning critics. Subversion and containment are the keywords here, drawn directly from the political vocabulary of the Cold War. They established the underlying ground of the Kafka debate and have helped to determine our understanding of Kafka and *Das Schloß* down to the present day.

Chapter three takes up the fate of *Das Schloß* during the sixties and early seventies. It was a time no less shaped by Cold War preoccupations of the fifties, even though readings of Kafka's work were less candidly social and political. Containment functioned by bracketing political and social issues in favor of formal ones. Critical attention falls on Kafka's mastery and manipulation of narrative perspective, his complex exploration of literary irony, and his renewal of parable as a modern literary form. From the perspective of cultural criticism, the emphasis on form was in part a retreat from earlier social and ethical criticism but also a counterbalance to attacks from orthodox Marxists of the Eastern bloc who denigrated Kafka's fiction as a symptom of

Western decadence, the opposite of their supposedly wholesome socialist realism. Naysayers in the East, liberalizers such as Milan Kundera and the Czech literary critic Eduard Goldstücker, were dealt with harshly by the authorities. Their Kafka served as an icon of the Prague Spring with which they were both associated. As a symbol of intellectual and creative freedom, he was a challenge to the status quo, a subversive threat that Soviet cultural authorities and their functionaries in the satellite states were eager to contain.

In the United States the new waves of structural and then poststructural criticism gradually came into competition with forms of cultural criticism that arose during the mid-seventies and have flourished during the eighties and into the present. In Kafka criticism the intellectual presence of Adorno has been strong. His seminal *Prisms*, a book of essays in cultural criticism, appeared in English in 1967. It includes his essay of 1953 on Kafka, which was discernibly influenced by Walter Benjamin's reflections. While Adorno's critical theory is only one strand of cultural criticism that has gained currency, it was particularly important for Kafka criticism because it showed in an exemplary way that social meanings could be wrested from the seeming detachment of Kafka's autonomous texts. Indeed, for Adorno, autonomy is the precondition of serious social comment in modern fiction and art.

But Adorno's negative dialectic is not the only means whereby critics have rescued social meaning from the castle. Chapter four charts the renewed prestige of contextual criticism in Kafka studies and *Schloß* criticism. The trend of the eighties toward an interest in the way literary texts are imbedded in the social, historical, ethnic and religious contexts from which they emerged has had a strong impact on the ways in which *Das Schloß* has been understood. Above all, Kafka's confrontation with the complexities of Central European Jewish identity as it may be reflected in *Das Schloß* has emerged as central. But contextualism often proceeds at the cost of aesthetic specificity. In the final chapter I advance a view of *Das Schloß* that likewise emphasizes Kafka's confrontation with Jewish thought and identity, but that is rooted more deeply in Kafka's idiosyncratic imaginative life than in the broad context of his generation's shared intellectual life.

2: Kafka in the Weimar Era

TUBERCULOSIS EMANCIPATED KAFKA, in a sense, because it gave him the freedom from job and family that he had always craved. The doctors first diagnosed his condition in 1917. Seriously weakened as a result of his gathering illness, Kafka was obliged virtually to devote himself to caring for his health. When his symptoms took an especially ugly turn in January 1922, his doctor sent him for a rest cure to Spindlermühle, a winter health resort in the mountains near the Polish border. It was here, probably, that Kafka began writing *Das Schloß*, which he continued to work on steadily during the winter, spring, and summer of 1922.

His brief stay at Spindlermühle did no good for his condition, though. On his return to Prague in mid-February he found his health little improved and decided to apply for an extended leave of absence from his post at the Workers' Accident Insurance Institute. His employer agreed to release him until June. Still, Kafka soon understood that even several more months of rest would not make any real difference in his steadily worsening condition.

Death and disease had long been a preoccupation of his imagination, though now they took on a new, more immediate meaning. He had particularly enjoyed the death scenes he had written, as a diary entry relates (December 13, 1914), because they involved seducing the reader's emotions while he, the author, stood apart and reveled in the scene of imaginary death. The imaginative act itself provided him with a sense of ironic detachment. Writing in general served to detach him from lived reality. His nocturnal bouts of writing had always been an escape hatch through which he could take refuge from responsibilities: his job, his duties to his family, the real and imagined demands of his father, the expectations of the various women to whom he engaged himself at various times.

Kafka was what might be called a serial fiancé. The balky bridegroom would go as far as official engagement, but no further. The prospect of marriage and its connubial duties simultaneously attracted him and filled him with dread. The act of writing was a private space he could crawl into and be alone, free, at least for a while, from the obligations of daily life. But as he himself frequently noted, there was something unwholesome and deathlike about his withdrawal into his imagination. The freedom he achieved through writing closed him off from the more social, more humane pleasures: sex, food and drink, and music, not to mention active involvement in family and community.

He believed his imaginative accomplishments and even his failures had been attained at the cost of a guilty asceticism, a torture that did not lead directly to death itself but to the infinitely worse "eternal torments" of the process of dying. Histrionic self-dramatization came as naturally to Kafka as writing. But the onset of a fatal illness unexpectedly threatened to fulfill his most lurid phantasies of banishment from the human world, visions of pain and death. "Was ich gespielt habe," he wrote in the summer of 1922 to Max Brod, "wird wirklich geschehn": what he had only been playing at in his fiction would now become reality.

Kafka requested an early retirement from the insurance company, and his request was granted in July 1922. He spent most of the summer at his sister Ottla's rented two-room cottage in the southern Bohemian countryside near the village of Planá. He stayed there with Ottla, her husband Josef David (who was present only some of the time), their daughter Vera, and a maid. Though he complained about the noise even here, for schoolchildren from the city were also on holiday nearby, he continued writing his novel until August, when another severe "breakdown," as he put it, interrupted his work on the castle narrative for good.

Almost nothing is known about how the novel took shape intellectually and imaginatively. He worked at the same time on some shorter pieces, including "Erstes Leid" (First Sorrow), "Ein Hungerkünstler" (A Hunger Artist), and "Forschungen eines Hundes" (Investigations of a Dog). Brod has plausibly suggested that the nineteenth-century Czech classic *Babčka* (Little Grandmother), by Božena Němcov{, may have supplied Kafka with the basic framework of *Das Schloß*. Kafka certainly knew the book, for he mentions it in his letters, and it is in any case well known to literate speakers of Czech. It deals with tension between the nobles on a German estate and the people of the nearby Czech village. Its configuration of peasants, scheming servants, and bureaucrats somewhat resembles Kafka's arrangement. Even so, the proposition remains speculative and, even if true, not very revealing.

Kafka himself offers little information about his novel's background and genesis. His letters and diaries seldom mention *Das Schloß*. We know that in March 1922 he read the first chapter aloud to Brod, who edited the long fragment for publication after Kafka's death in 1924.

Kurt Wolff published the first edition in Munich in 1926, and in 1930 the English translation appeared. The French version followed eight years later.

By the time the novel became available in print in German, Kafka was already known among the cognoscenti for the shorter works he had published during his lifetime — tales, parables, and aphorisms. Various pieces had appeared in literary journals, and he had seen three collections into print himself: *Betrachtung* (1913), *Ein Landarzt* (1919), and *Ein Hungerkünstler* (1924). In addition, three individual tales had also appeared as single volumes: *Die Verwandlung* (1915), *Das Urteil* (1916), and *In der Strafkolonie* (1919). Brod, whom Kafka had entrusted with most of his posthumous papers (and who, according to Brod himself, was supposed to burn them), saw to it that *Der Prozeß* appeared in print quickly. It was published in Berlin in 1925.

The appearance of *Das Schloß* in 1926, then, was an intellectual event of some importance, at least in some of the more discriminating circles. It is hardly an exaggeration to say that almost immediately a struggle for control of Kafka's intellectual legacy broke out. Max Brod laid first claim to a definitive understanding of Kafka's meaning, first by virtue of his long and intimate relationship with Kafka (they had been close friends since 1902) but also because he had literal control of the works themselves. He appended an afterword to the first edition of *Das Schloß* in which he not only explains the circumstances of the unfinished work's publication but also stakes his claim to an authoritative interpretation. A year earlier he had refrained from interpretive commentary in his edition of *Der Prozeß*, but — alarmed by the public response to that work and what he considered to be the "crass misinterpretations" of it — Brod felt it necessary to undertake a preemptive hermeneutic strike on behalf of his own views.

In it Brod links Kafka to German classicism, presenting K. to the novel's first readers as the modern Faust. Unlike his Goethean predecessor, the Kafkan Faust strives for divine grace instead of knowledge. However, the divine and the human, the castle and the village, are irreconcilable, says Brod. He argues too that Kierkegaard's *Fear and Trembling* had influenced Kafka decisively, supplying him with the idea that an unbridgeable abyss severs the human from the divine. Thus K.'s attempts to establish himself in the village with a wife and a job aim at a spiritual redemption that he will never achieve — or even fail to achieve. The clarity of a clean failure would be too positive an upshot for Kafka.

Brod also reports that Kafka once told him of plans for a conclusion to the novel: on his deathbed the would-be surveyor, exhausted and defeated, with the village people gathered round him, would receive a message from the castle denying his actual right to live in the village yet also permitting him to stay, owing to certain unspecified circumstances. We must assume that Brod's report of Kafka's intention is reasonably reliable. However, we must also assume that Brod was most likely to report whatever information conformed to his own strong opinions about Kafka's intentions. As Kafka's friend, executor, and editor, Brod offered his views to Kafka's growing audience as authoritative. And his religiously grounded interpretation largely had the desired effects. With few exceptions, the contemporaneous book reviewers found Brod's afterword persuasive and followed its interpretation.

Nor was Brod one to let Kafka's reputation develop on its own. He continued to work assiduously to promote his friend's stature, or his own version of it, among the German intelligentsia. When in 1931 he and his younger associate, Heinz Politzer, brought out a volume of posthumous Kafka writings under the title *Beim Bau der Chinesischen Mauer* (The Great Wall of China), Brod engineered a public declaration of Kafka's greatness that was signed by six of the era's best known and most respected writers: Martin Buber, André Gide, Hermann Hesse, Heinrich Mann, Thomas Mann, and Franz Werfel. It appeared in the *Berliner Tagblatt* on May 31, 1931, and was couched as an appeal to the reading public to support the publication of Kafka's works. Implied is the necessity of an intellectual and moral commitment from the reading public to buy expensive books during a time of uncontrollable inflation:

> The posthumous writings of Franz Kafka are now being made available through a large-scale publishing effort. The two volumes — which will contain numerous unpublished tales and sketches, a cycle of aphorisms, excerpts from books and diaries as well as biographical documentation — should, if they find favor with the reading public, mark the beginning of a complete edition of his works. Such an edition would include all of his published works along with supplementary material from his posthumous papers and works that are out of print. Kafka's greatness is becoming clearer and clearer in Germany, in England, and in France. If the three posthumous novels have taught us to see in Kafka — the man we had admired as a master of language and of the miniature forms — also a novelist comparable to the greatest, and an implacable shaper and interpreter of the age, then we now confront

the surprise that the writer's personal documents show him to be a severe and exemplary figure struggling from the profound depths of his religious consciousness. For this reason we call attention to the edition of his collected works that is now in preparation; it is an intellectual deed of inordinate dimensions. Its importance now, in these days of a confusion that distracts the mind from what is of the essence, is clear to all those whom Kafka's word addresses.

Kafka's public image, and with it the reputation of his castle novel, was shaped by the climate of economic, social, political and religious crisis that was mounting in the late twenties and early thirties. It must be noted, too, that by endorsing Brod's text, the famous writers were also endorsing his reading of Kafka as a fundamentally religious artist.

In his introductory note to the English translation in 1930, Edwin Muir informs the reader that "*The Castle* is, like the *Pilgrim's Progress*, a religious allegory." And in 1940, when Thomas Mann wrote his "Homage" to Kafka that still serves as a foreword to one edition of *The Castle*, he too held fast to a religious interpretation. Mann's "Homage" owes much to Brod's afterword: "For it is plain that regular life in a community, the ceaseless struggle to become a 'native,' is simply a technique for improving K.'s relations with the Castle, or rather to set up relations with it: to attain nearer, in other words, to God and to a state of grace." But it is not entirely clear whether K. wants to become a native or whether it merely suits his purposes to appear so.

There is little reason to believe that K. wants to become one of the villagers. The abrasive and manipulative wayfarer who claims to be a surveyor summoned by the castle expresses no fondness for and little solidarity with the village and its people. And it is even less clear that Kafka intended the castle authorities to be understood as instances of the divine. Mann's own remarks suggest the opposite when he turns his attention to Kafka's satirical sense of humor:

> This is what makes Kafka a religious humorist: that he does not, as literature is prone to do, treat the incomprehensible, the incommensurable, the humanly unassessable transcendent world in a style either grandiose, ecstatic, or hyper-emotional. No, he sees and depicts it as an Austrian 'department'; as a magnification of a petty, obstinate, unaccountable bureaucracy; a mammoth establishment of documents and procedures, headed by some darkly responsible official hierarchy.

If Mann's assessment is correct, Kafka's aim must have been to unmask the divine as "a petty, obstinate, unaccountable bureaucracy." On the other hand, he might just as well have intended the opposite: to magnify with ironic intent the famously shapeless and inefficient bureaucracy of Austria to quasi-divine proportions. In either case the result is comic, but not religious or mythopoeic.

Certainly religion and myth were in the air during the Weimar era. Without apparent recourse to Brod's interpretation, Hermann Broch, too, sensed a religious dimension in Kafka, though in a different way. In the 1936 essay "James Joyce und die Gegenwart" (James Joyce and the Present Age) Broch ranks Kafka and Joyce together as the two most important literary voices of the era. He sees in their fiction the signs of a return to mythic totality. By that Broch means that their imaginative achievement is such that it symbolically embodies the whole of the modern era, straining toward (but not attaining) the condition of myth.

Broch never offered a detailed analysis of *Das Schloß*, but his attitude toward Kafka is characteristic of the era and its "hunger for wholeness," a phrase that is ironically apt for the author of "Ein Hungerkünstler." The terrible state of the Austrian and German economies, the disarray of their broken, seemingly unreformable political cultures, and the low public morale after the debacle of the First World War created a sense of historical failure and spiritual void that German novelists explored with great insistence. Intellectual life in the Weimar Era and its Austrian equivalent, the First Republic, was conspicuously preoccupied with the theme of returning to some supposedly lost wholeness.[1] A central aspect of finding the way back gave great force, in literature and politics, to the theme of redemption.

As a German-speaking Jew surrounded by Czech nationalists and Austrian Germans in an increasingly anti-Semitic mood, Kafka suffered acutely from the hunger for wholeness. He regretted the half-hearted Judaism of his upbringing and reproached his father bitterly for it in the famous "Letter to his Father." He admired the tradition and authenticity of the unassimilated eastern Jews. He saw in their way of life a cultural wholeness denied to him because he was brought up with little sense of devotion to Jewish religion, history, or custom and with no Yiddish or Hebrew.

For obvious reasons, Zionism should have had an obvious appeal to Kafka, as it did to many of his closest friends, including Max Brod, Felix Weltsch, and Hugo Bergmann. It is true that in later life Kafka read

---

[1] The phrase is Peter Gay's, "The Hunger for Wholeness: Trials of Modernity," *Weimar Culture: The Outsider as Insider* (New York: Harper and Row, 1968), 70–101.

about it eagerly, though he had rejected it when he was younger, and that he even took up the study of Hebrew. That Kafka seriously pondered the nature and meaning of Judaism and his own Jewishness is beyond question. Nevertheless, the evidence suggests that his intellect was too corrosively skeptical, his natural cast of mind too ironic, his sense of belatedness too laming for him to invest any realistic hope in religious salvation or the utopian — or what at that time must have seemed utopian — dream of a Jewish state. As much as Kafka wanted to belong among the Jews, perhaps even among the Zionists, he felt himself a permanent, irredeemable exile:

> Ich habe von den Erfordernissen des Lebens gar nichts mitgebracht, so viel ich weiß, sondern nur die allgemeine menschliche Schwäche. Mit dieser — in dieser Hinsicht ist es eine riesenhafte Kraft — habe ich das Negative meiner Zeit, die mir ja sehr nahe ist, die ich nie zu bekämpfen, sondern gewissermaßen zu vertreten das Recht habe, kräftig aufgenommen. An dem geringen Positiven so wie an dem äußersten, zum Positiven umkippenden Negativen, hatte ich keinen ererbten Anteil. Ich bin nicht von der allerdings schon schwer sinkenden Hand des Christentums ins Leben geführt worden wie Kierkegaard und habe nicht den letzten Zipfel des davonfliegenden jüdischen Gebetsmantels noch gefangen wie die Zionisten. Ich bin Ende oder Anfang. (*Hochzeitsvorbereitungen auf dem Lande*, 1953:120.)

> [I brought with me none of life's prerequisites, as far as I know, only the general human weakness. Along with it — and in this regard it is a gigantic power — I have absorbed mightily the negativity of my era, a negativity that is very close to me and that I never fought but that to a certain extent I have the right to represent. Neither to the era's meager positivity nor to the most extreme negation that tips over into the positive do I have a birthright. I was not, like Kierkegaard, escorted into life by the heavily sinking hand of Christianity; nor was I able, like the Zionists, to catch hold of the last tip of the Jewish prayer shawl as it flew past and away. I am last or first.]

He ardently longed for solidarity and community, but he never dared to actually believe in them, not least of all because he longed just as ardently for the solitude and silence that were the precondition of his writing. But even his writing withheld from him the limited access to redemption that he once derived from it. In a letter of July 5, 1922, he wrote to Brod of his despair: "Ich habe mich durch das Schreiben nicht losgekauft. Mein Leben lang bin ich gestorben, und nun werde ich wirklich sterben" [My writing has not bought off my death. I've been dying all my life, and now I'll really die]. There is no talk here, at a time when he was still in the middle of composing *Das Schloß*, of religion or grace, transcendence, or redemption. Writing had failed him.

Nevertheless, Max Brod's influential attempt to represent K. as the image of enlightened modern man trying to reconcile himself with his god, his calling, and his community has an obvious appeal, one that must have been particularly strong for the Weimar era audience. Anchored in an intellectual setting that was in many ways dominated by the hope for a redemption of some sort — whether political, social, religious, cultural, or some combination thereof — Brod's interpretation made sense. However, Brod's own sensibility was more confident, less skeptical than his friend's. Other, less sanguine spirits offered darker readings of K. and his castle, readings tied more closely to the secular than to the religious imagination.

Reviewing the book for the *Frankfurter Zeitung* in November 1926, Siegfried Kracauer sensibly objects that the castle is too hellish a place to be identified with the divine. In his view the novel pivots on K.'s inability to discover truth. K.'s dilemma embodies the general modern condition of being locked out of authentic knowledge, which Kracauer refers to as a dislocation between human beings and truth. His Kafka reveals a world that truth has abandoned, and consequently one in which history has come to an end (a proposition that opens a potentially rich perspective on the novel's peculiarly static sense of time). In a world devoid of a deeper truth, things and events mean only themselves; they do not point to something behind or beyond them. Even the commonplace certainties of daily life — the recording of an official statement, delivering a message, and the like — become mysterious, intractable problems.

Truth has vanished and left anxiety in its place. Kafka's world, suggests Kracauer, is the opposite of the one revealed in fairy tales, in which a great and all-embracing order of things finds continual reaffirmation. It is this truth that Kafka's world lacks. In his version of the world, the witch simply eats Hansel and Gretel. No doubt Kracauer, too, felt the hunger for wholeness. But the image of the witch puts quite a different spin on the phrase. He was less willing than Brod, and the critics who accepted his views, to succumb to romantic yearnings.[2]

---

[2] For a representative selection of responses, see the reviews that Jürgen Born has reprinted in his *Franz Kafka: Kritik und Rezeption 1924–1938* (Frankfurt am Main: S. Fischer, 1983), 135–84.

If Brod and Kracauer represent the two poles of Kafka criticism in the thirties, then Walter Benjamin is the figure most precariously balanced between the choice of a theologically framed understanding of Kafka and a view of him that is secular and critical. Kracauer sent him a copy of the *Schloß* review in 1927, and Benjamin wrote back that he had not yet read the novel but was looking forward to it. In fact, at that time Benjamin had not yet read much Kafka at all, but by 1931 he had studied carefully all that was available and had in the process amassed a considerable body of notes and commentary. His store of observations culminated in a 1931 radio talk called "Franz Kafka: Beim Bau der Chinesischen Mauer" and in his famous essay of 1934 "Franz Kafka."

Benjamin's Kafka essay, commissioned by the *Jüdische Rundschau* in observance of the tenth anniversary of the writer's death, marks an important crossroads in the development of Kafka criticism. It appeared after the advent of the Third Reich, at a time when Benjamin and almost all of his friends and intellectual associates were in exile. The latent political content of Kafka's fiction, and not least its varied figurations of exile, such as the castle's K., demanded sustained exegesis. The two principal influences on Benjamin at the time represent the two poles that simultaneously attracted him and that dominated the intellectual climate of the Weimar era. At one end of the spectrum (in Danish exile) stood Bertolt Brecht, who then regarded Kafka, as Benjamin was pleased to discover, as a genuine Bolshevist writer. At the other end of the spectrum was the idiosyncratic Zionist and adept of Jewish mysticism Gershom Scholem, in Jerusalem, who understood Kafka's fiction as a modern transformation and renewal of ancient Jewish mysticism.

The difficulties of combining these two points of orientation are obvious. But Benjamin yokes them together in characteristically imaginative and cunningly dialectical image. In his attempts to write about Kafka he presents himself as an archer struggling to draw back the string on a heavy bow: "Hier habe ich es mit zwei Enden zugleich zu tun, nämlich dem politischen und dem mystischen." The tension between the two ends of the bow is what will give force to the missile — the essay he is trying to write. Benjamin had hoped to write a book about Kafka, but because he was unable to find a publisher who would give him a much needed advance on it, he had to abandon the idea.

So the 1934 piece that appeared in the *Jüdische Rundschau*, which was only about half of what Benjamin had written (it omitted the sections called "Ein Kinderbild" and "Sancho Pansa"), remained his only substantial writing on Kafka to appear in print before fuller editions of his work began to appear after the war. In its entirety the essay is challenging. In private circulation among his friends it became the subject of much stimulating criticism and discussion.[3] Brecht strongly disliked it, bluntly telling Benjamin that it was obscure and, worse yet, in its obscurity unwittingly "advanced the cause of Jewish fascism." Scholem, along with Werner Kraft, Theodor Adorno, and Max Horkheimer, had more productive remarks of praise and criticism to make. But in the long run Benjamin too was dissatisfied with the essay. In a 1938 essay-letter to Scholem, which is now customarily printed with the essay as a supplement, Benjamin takes issue with himself.

Still, it is a remarkable document for its scattering of piercing insights and for the way that it embodies a fundamental conflict of Weimar intellectual life. Benjamin is not able to hammer together a coherent view of Kafka's writing, as he freely conceded in his letters, probably because the clash between mysticism and politics forbids it, but along the way he makes connections and limns insights that remain compelling. Benjamin calls articulate attention to Kafka's use of gesture; to the theme of anamnesis ("In Kafka's tales forgottenness is the vessel from which an inexhaustible spirit world emerges to seek the light."); and to the archaic, anarchic "swampworld" in which many of his characters (women, children, soldiers, barbarians) and feelings (guilt, shame) seem to originate. Above all, Benjamin writes about Kafka in a language of arresting images, which, like Kafka's own language of image and gesture, tantalizes the imagination but seldom can be resolved into the kind of flat-footed "position" that Brecht evidently expected him to produce.

Benjamin's Kafka essays are important too for the writers they influenced later on, people like Adorno and Hannah Arendt. During the war, when Arendt wrote her Kafka essay for *Partisan Review* (another commemoration, this time marking the twentieth anniversary of the writer's death), she resolved the tension between mysticism and politics in favor of politics. Hence she calls the essay a "revaluation," laying her emphasis on the political and social meaning she finds in Kafka, and especially in the castle novel. That her essay appeared in *Partisan*

---

[3] The origins and development of Benjamin's work on Kafka are traced in the commentary supplied by Benjamin's editors: *Gesammelte Werke*, eds. Rolf Tiedemann and Hermann Schwepphäuser, vol. II/3 (Frankfurt am Main: Suhrkamp, 1977), 1153–1276.

Review, a journal which by then had become focused on the interplay of American liberalism with political theory, social theory, and modernism in art and literature, is itself indicative.[4]

Arendt's Kafka is above all the author of *Das Schloß.* She sees its protagonist as a rebel against unseen forces of oppression and domination. He insists on his rights from the castle and emerges in her reading as a champion of human rights in general: "K.'s stubborn singleness of purpose . . . opens the eyes of some of the villagers; his behavior teaches them that human rights are worth fighting for, that the rule of the Castle is not divine law and, consequently, can be attacked. He makes them see that 'men who suffered our own kind of experiences, who are beset by our kind of fear, . . . who tremble at every knock at the door cannot see things straight.' And they add: 'How lucky we are that you came to us!'" Of course it would be just as easy to claim a messianic purport for this passage. The Hebrew word for surveyor (*mashoah*), as Evelyn Torton Beck has pointed out, is almost identical to the word for messiah (*mashiah*). Kafka knew enough Hebrew to know that.

Still, in 1944 there was every reason to think through and accentuate the politically subversive, antitotalitarian aspect of Kafka's fiction rather than its mystical or religious side. The Nazi culture police had proscribed his works, and if Kafka had lived long enough he would likely have perished — along with family and friends — in Hitler's death camps. His political credentials would seem beyond doubt. On the other hand, Kafka had been conspicuously apolitical during his lifetime. His inclination toward socialism and Zionism was casual, and the evidence of his fiction is ambiguous.

Obviously Kafka's work had its detractors, especially on the left. The orthodox Marxist critics condemned Kafka as a symptom of bourgeois cultural decay in the late capitalist era. The non-Marxist critic who explored the perhaps dubious side of Kafka's achievement most acutely was the independent cultural critic Günther Stern, who later changed his name to Günther Anders. He was one of Kafka's early readers, so when he was asked to lecture on a contemporary writer in Paris in 1934 (as a part of a job application for teaching German), he

---

[4] "Liberalism — not the 19th-century ideology or social theology of the laissez-faire which was already moribund before the First World War — but liberalism as an intellectual temper, as faith in intelligence, as a tradition of the free market of ideas," writes Sidney Hook, *Partisan Review* 10 (1943): 3.

agreed to speak on Kafka. In the lecture he warned his audience — which included Hannah Arendt, who was his wife at the time (they separated in 1936), and Walter Benjamin — against what he regarded as a perniciously pseudoreligious, pseudopolitical Kafka fashion among intellectuals in France.

During the mid-forties, while he was teaching aesthetics at the New School for Social Research in New York City, Anders expanded his essay. In 1947 he published a part of it under the title "Kafka — pro und contra," in *Die Neue Rundschau* and in *Commentary*. In 1951 the whole of it finally appeared in Germany as a book. In it Anders puts uncomfortable questions to Kafka's work. With the same concerns in mind that motivated Hannah Arendt's essay, he presses the question of freedom, laying heavy emphasis on Kafka's perhaps communitarian ideals, which Anders views skeptically as the writer's "thirst for total belonging." He asks what the meaning may be of Kafka's preoccupation with dissolving the individual into some larger communal organism, not only in *Das Schloß*, in the Josephine story, "Bericht für eine Akademie," and in "Beim Bau der Chinesischen Mauer," but also in Kafka's odd romance with the idea of Eastern Jewry's greater authenticity and consequent moral superiority over supposedly rootless, inauthentic Western Jewry.

Anders argues that this sense of impoverishment and failure instills in Kafka's fiction the motif of bad conscience. In this representative passage he considers K.'s opportunistic acquiescence in the castle's moral squalor:

> K. strives to comply with all regulations, to assimilate them inwardly and even to justify the immoral demands of those who rule. In order to present this 'problem of justification' bluntly, Kafka represents those who rule as 'evil powers': and the efforts of the newcomer as a kind of conscientious accommodation (*Gleichschaltung*) to evil, by means of which K. does not take evil for good, but is simply willing to acquiesce in. The consciousness of not being able to acknowledge orders as moral is a motif of bad conscience. All of Kafka's philosophical aphorisms prove that Kafka not only describes the justification but also affirms and even attempts this dubious undertaking. Even Kafka is, in a certain sense, a moralist of conformism (*Gleichschaltung*). (Anders 1947)

Those are hard words, and certainly overstated because of Anders's understandable preoccupation with the problem of conformism in the Nazi era, but they are not without basis. Even if he exaggerates the *Gleichschaltung* angle, he is right about K.'s dubious moral character, a point not much in evidence in Kafka criticism of the forties, perhaps because of the influence of Albert Camus's antiheroes and his own claim that Kafka's are similar to them (Camus 1942). Unlike those who felt uncritically inclined to celebrate K. as a existential or political rebel-hero, Anders takes the text seriously and reads it carefully. Still, Anders's position has found few adherents. His K. is a self-seeking opportunist, a prophet of conformism and social resignation.

Anders goes on to speculate interestingly about Kafka's dying wish for Max Brod to burn the unpublished manuscripts and other writings. Anders does not question the truth of the request, but he does offer a powerful explanation for it. He suspects that moral, not aesthetic, reasons underlay Kafka's request. Kafka understood that his writing was aesthetically of the highest order, but *only* aesthetically. Rather like Hermann Broch's Virgil, Anders's Kafka doubts not his artistic genius but its human worth. Though Anders does not mention her, he might have called Josefine, the mouse singer, as a witness for his case. While the mouse folk hold her in high regard, Kafka's narrator makes it clear that she and her art will both be forgotten, and that this is as it should be. If what Brod said about Kafka's dying request is true, then we must assume that Kafka would have been happy for his works, like Josefine and her voice, to slip quietly and entirely from public memory.

So Anders, curmudgeonly and uncompromising moralist that he is, is not anti-Kafka, or at least not entirely. His Kafka is a writer divided against himself, a novelist whose fiction, however consummate its artistry, embodies a failure of will and a loss of nerve on the part of the Western, liberal imagination. Precisely this issue would underlie the next phase of Kafka and *Schloß* criticism during the Cold War.

3: Kafka and the Cold War

KAKFA'S ASCENT INTO the canon of American and European classics coincides significantly with the Cold War. Though the terror and final defeat of National Socialism are connected in an obvious way to Kafka's reputation, it may be less obvious how the McCarthy era in the United States and the Adenauer era of restoration in the Federal Republic have helped to create and sustain a certain image of Kafka and *Das Schloß* in the public imagination.

As the postwar confrontation between the United States and the Soviet Union took on recognizable contours, George Kennan's famous essay "The Sources of Soviet Conduct," which appeared in the journal *Foreign Affairs* in 1947, mapped the terrain. He founded the basic strategy of American policy by defining the need to oppose and contain Communist subversion at home and around the world. And in shaping American policy, Kennan also indirectly helped to determine the intellectual climate and establish the terms of cultural debate (Suchoff 1994:9–39).

The mood of fear and suspicion that grew at American universities during the McCarthy era was not subtle. It was the era of "loyalty oaths." The congressional hearings on un-American activities had a chilling effect on writers, filmmakers, and intellectuals that is well known. But I want to argue now that the Cold War mentality also had a bearing on the course of development of Kafka criticism and that the terms *subversion* and *containment,* coined for use in political discourse, also found their way into the literary discussion about modernism in general and about Kafka in particular.

K. in Manhattan

Let us turn first to the situation in the United States. At the most basic level the Cold War image of Soviet totalitarianism dovetailed with the earlier interpretations of Kafka as the prophet of Nazi totalitarianism. Hannah Arendt's reading of Kafka in *Partisan Review* (1944) was discussed in the previous chapter. If her understanding of Kafka as an antitotalitarian novelist held true for the era of the Nazi threat, then her thesis would be just as appealing during the era of the gulag. The important difference is simply that during the forties Kafka was not so well known. During the fifties he emerged along with the other great modernists as a classic to be read in university classrooms.

The Cold War environment, then, gave a continued and enlarged political meaning to modernist alienation and cultural malaise. Kafka's K. (to name the obvious example) could still be understood as a rebel against the forces of dehumanization and oppression, with Stalinism replacing Nazism on the immediate horizon. It can hardly be surprising that, in the cultural setting of Cold War politics, postwar American intellectuals established a canon for themselves that favored an aesthetics of revolt. Nor is it surprising that they displaced the revolt from politics onto art. Many of the New York intellectuals, for example, had been radical leftists in the twenties and thirties. By the forties most had given up the thought of radical political transformation in the United States and left their ties to Marxism and socialism far behind (Wald 1987:226–63). The modernist rebellion was safely apolitical, or just political enough to remain savory. It was a revolt against the prevailing style, only symbolically a revolt against the status quo, and included Melville and Hawthorne, Dostoyevsky and Proust, Dickens and Joyce, and — at the outer limit of admissibility — Franz Kafka.

A key figure in American literary criticism at this decisive moment of canon formation was Lionel Trilling. From the perspective of Kafka's reputation he is more important than the New Critics, who in any case leaned more toward poetry, because Trilling took for granted what he called "the inevitably intimate if not always obvious connection between literature and politics." The phrase comes from his seminal collection of essays, *The Liberal Imagination*. Published in 1950, it was an unofficial manifesto that sought to establish a self-aware and uncomplacent American liberalism as a cornerstone of literary understanding. Toward this end Trilling put together a selection of essays meant to exemplify "a criticism which has at heart the interests of liberalism."

The term *liberalism* is roomy and imprecise enough in general usage, and unfortunately Trilling never gets around to defining what he means by it. Some of the time it refers to the liberal intellectuals of the left during the thirties and forties who had consciously or unconsciously acquiesced in Stalinism. These are the fallen liberals, the ones who lack the morally alert imagination that Trilling intends to return to American intellectual life. In its positive sense, the term as he uses it does not refer to a doctrine of specific positions and ideas. Rather, his liberalism might best be understood to mean a cultural and political *temperament* that emphasizes the free exercise of critical intelligence against the forces of conformity.

Trilling's intellectual and moral stake in literary modernism arose from what he and his peers perceived to be the intrinsically critical force of modernist narrative proper but also that of its nineteenth-century precursors. In his essay "The Dickens of Our Day," Trilling aligns Kafka with Dickens on the grounds that both were social critics and, interestingly, critics of the family: "To read Kafka's life and works under the parental relations of, say, *Dombey and Son*, of *David Copperfield* and of *Little Dorrit* (this last especially pertinent with its overshadowing prisons and its Circumlocution Office in which no official may ever give an answer) is to understand the perfect continuity of the twentieth century with the nineteenth." No doubt Trilling has a point. No reader of *Das Schloß* literate in European fiction can fail to hear echoes of *Little Dorrit* and *Bleak House* in the parts of Kafka's work as a whole that satirize modern bureaucracy and legalistic rigmarole. Still, we also sense Trilling straining to make his case. There is more that separates Kafka from Dickens than holds them together.

But Trilling does not rest his case with the similarity to Dickens. There are other precursors. In an essay called "Hawthorne in Our Time" Trilling ponders the rise of Hawthorne from relative obscurity into the modernist canon — that is, the nineteenth-century canon reformulated from the perspective of modernism. In his view, the powerful impression that Kafka made on American intellectuals during the forties and fifties contributed to the positive reassessment of Hawthorne's dark works. Yet in this essay, Trilling is plainly ill at ease with Kafka's intellectual and moral prestige:

> The idea 'I did something wrong' is of course omnipresent, but that means only 'I did not do the required thing, which the Law demands; and therefore I shall be punished.' What intransigence of imagination is needed to conceive man's spiritual life as having no discernible connection with morality! (Trilling 1965:174)

The moral ambiguity of life below the castle is a case in point. As Günther Anders had already pointed out before Trilling, K. grasps the immorality of the castle but responds by merely trying to turn it to his own advantage. Frieda, Barnabas, even little Hans are pawns in his duel with the castle. Morality in itself is of little or no consequence to him. He is an immoralist.

In the wake of Nietzsche and Gide (and going back ultimately to Goethe) "immoralism" is a basic theme of the modernist imagination, and its larger implications clash with Trilling's liberal agenda.

> And if . . . we name those writers who, by the general consent of the most serious criticism, . . . are to be thought of as the monumental figures of our time, we see that to these writers the liberal ideology has been at best a matter of indifference. Proust, Joyce, Lawrence, Eliot, Yeats, Mann (in his creative work), Kafka, Rilke, Gide — all have their own love of justice and the good life, but not for one of them does it take the form of a love of the ideas and emotions which liberal democracy, as known by our educated class, has declared respectable. (Trilling 1950:98)

With these sobering words, Trilling shifts the burden of liberalism onto the critic's shoulders, since the writers have not proved themselves to be politically reliable. It is up to the critic to resolve the tension between illiberal genius and the values "that liberal democracy has declared respectable." Trilling, then, admires Kafka's imaginative achievement with some reluctance. In fact, Kafka marks the outer boundary of the liberal imagination and its canon, in his view. This is odd, considering that Kafka's fiction, more than that of any of his peers, embodies the subversive character of art that Trilling otherwise celebrates as a part of literature's social responsibility to question and probe the status quo.

Why did the great German modernist, who is also the great Jewish modernist, fail to become a centerpiece of Trilling's liberal canon? Why did Trilling never devote a major essay to Kafka? There are no doubt many reasons, but the one that bears on the present inquiry has to do with the subversive aspect of modernism. "Any critic of literature of the modern age," writes Trilling in the preface to *Beyond Culture*,

> will take virtually for granted the adversary intention, the actually subversive intention, that characterizes modern writing — he will perceive its clear purpose of detaching the reader from habits of thought and feeling that the larger culture imposes, of giving him a ground and a vantage point from which to judge and condemn, and perhaps revise, the culture that produced him.

Trilling hews to the optimistic view that literature has the power to contribute significantly toward the redemption of modern society. His commitment to the liberal, enlightened approach to literature and criticism, coupled with his advocacy of the frequently illiberal modernists, puts Trilling between a rock and a hard place. He found himself forced to defend the one against the other.

In an acute commentary of 1950, R. W. B. Lewis noted that Trilling's argument in *The Liberal Imagination* is absorbed with "containing the enemy, in the cold war it believes will always be with us" (317). *Containment* is the key word here, and the reasons the Cold War will always be with us are Freudian, spelled out in *Civilization and its Discontents*. Human nature is at bottom illiberal, continually at war with reason and the civilizing impulse. Disappointed and disaffected by the leftist politics in the Stalin era, Trilling and other New York intellectuals abandoned the pro-Soviet positions and Marxism of their early years. Doubly chastened by the era of Hitler and continued oppression of their Eastern European comrades under the regime of Stalin, America's Cold War liberals had become more skeptical about social progress and human perfectibility than they had been in the revolutionary twenties and thirties. The trauma of World War II, the incomparable horror of the Holocaust, then Stalinism, McCarthyism, and the possibility of nuclear destruction — all these factors pushed them into more conservative positions. Revolution in American society no longer seemed such a good idea. But literary tastes are more flexible than political realities. Revolution safely contained in literature remained appealing, as long as it was not *too* subversive.

Kafka was a borderline case, unlike, say, Ernst Jünger or Gottfried Benn. If his fiction represented a subversive force, then the liberal imagination would be able to contain it. Trilling admired Kafka's formidable imaginative achievement, yet he understood — and rightly so — that it posed a challenge, even a threat, to the liberal culture he thought literature and criticism ought to nourish. Whatever its artistic virtues, Kafka's fiction was not liberal in Trilling's sense. It radically questions the very "ground from which we judge and condemn"; and there can be little talk of Kafka's fiction "revising" the culture that produced it either. The culture that produced Kafka would probably have murdered him if he had lived long enough to enter the death camps with his family and friends.

Trilling's discontent with Kafka helps to clarify the hermeneutical background of the fifties and sixties. The clash between liberal ideals and Kafkan pessimism is an elemental aspect of the Kafka reception of the Cold War era, and it is also basic to understanding the underlying assumptions and motives that preceded specific readings of *Das Schloß*. It is a conflict that gives rise to questions that touch at the essence of Kafka's fiction. Does Kafka's fiction in general, and *Das Schloß* in par-

ticular, contain within its labyrinthine ironies a genuine critical and redemptive force, or does it belong to a dark, antiliberal, anti-
Enlightenment strain of the romantic tradition that reaches back to
Sade and de Maistre? After all, Janouch records that the author of "In
der Strafkolonie" thought of Sade as "der eigentliche Patron unserer
Zeit" (1951:78). If Kafka is the great guide into modern culture's
heart of darkness — our Dante, as Auden claimed — what he brings to
light is not good news.

In Adenauer's Germany

The German experience of the forties was nothing short of Sadean, but
that in no way helps to explain the Kafka boom in Germany after the
war. The larger reason has to do with the specific, liberal image of the
individual in conflict with the total authority represented by the court
in *Der Proceß* and by the castle in *Das Schloß*. Stalinist oppression in the
East and the outbreak of the Cold War on German soil, with its terrible consequences for the city of Berlin in particular, made Kafka seem
doubly prescient.

If the New York intellectuals can be taken as an indicator of the
mood of the sector of the American intelligentsia most likely to gravi-
tate toward Kafka, then a similar, probably even more powerful force
can be discerned in Gruppe '47. The writers and critics of this literary
forum did much to raise Kafka to a position of public prominence in
German letters. Kafka and other modernists, from Proust and Gide to
Joyce, Mann, and Faulkner, all belonged to the fraternity of writers
whose works had been blacklisted, banned, and burned by the Nazi
censors of the Reichsschrifttumskammer. These writers had to be recovered and reintegrated into the German imagination. The two names
among the modernists that came up over and over in meetings of
Gruppe '47 were Hemingway and Kafka, two novelists whose styles
pointed away from the kitsch of Nazified German letters (and away
from the discredited bourgeois tradition embodied in the fiction of
Thomas Mann) and toward, or so many hoped, a new, emphatically
antifascist German literature.

The famous "Zero Hour" of German fiction writing that the generation of '47 proclaimed was thus a crucial moment in the construction of the modernist canon. The writers and critics on the inside of
the circle (and it was hotly criticized by outsiders for its powerful
trendsetting function in German literary life) were unified above all by

the idea that German literature was bound by recent history and its classical tradition to become oppositional, antifascist, and antitotalitarian. To put the same point a different way, the common basis of affiliation that united this diverse group of intellectuals was in large part the liberal assumption that literature should be subversive.

While the group was supposed to be politically nonpartisan, its members generally inclined to one degree or another toward the liberal left. But with the restoration of capitalism and the rearmament of Adenauer's Federal Republic, along with increasingly repressive measures in the Eastern bloc, a rightward drift occurred. In addition, as the Economic Miracle began to pay dividends, creating a prosperous consumer culture in West Germany, writers found themselves drawn more deeply into the business of publishing and writing. Finally, Gruppe '47's programmatic distance from political engagement made its left-liberal image the object of ridicule from the radical left (especially the politicized students of the mid-sixties) and of suspicion from the conservative public at large. By its final meeting in the politically tumultuous year of 1967, Gruppe '47 had outlived itself.

In the fifties and early sixties, though, when Gruppe '47 was at the height of its prestige and influence, the name *Kafka* played a significant role in its meetings. In their efforts to remake German letters, they took Kafka's style, his persona, and his characteristic themes as a major point of departure. One of the group's most prominent novelists, Martin Walser, wrote a Tübingen dissertation on Kafka's narrative technique (1952). His pioneering study of Kafka's distinctive way of monopolizing narrative perspective (which his dissertation director, Friedrich Beißner, dubbed "Einsinnigkeit" in a series of related lectures) remains in print. Many of the group's other members also have written significant books, essays and literary works about Kafka: Klaus Wagenbach, Hans Mayer, Wolfgang Hildesheimer, Marcel Reich-Ranicki, Peter Weiss, Dieter Wellershof, and Reinhard Baumgart, to name only the most prominent.

But the response of novelist-critic Walter Jens is the most characteristic and revealing. Since the early fifties Jens has held an eminent position in German intellectual life not unlike the prestige that Trilling enjoyed during the fifties and sixties in the United States. Like Trilling, Jens writes for a wide audience, and, again like Trilling, he takes the unity of literature and politics to be of central importance to the polity. In a programmatic speech entitled "Literature: Possibilities and Limits," Jens wonders rhetorically why oppressive regimes have always gone to such extremes to eliminate subversive writing:

> The answer, as idealistic and abstract as it may sound, can only be this:
> it is the old, ineradicable fear that power feels in the presence of the
> mind and its subversive activity — a fear (and let the dogmatists take
> note) that reigns in both camps, among socialists and capitalists alike.
> (1976:84)

The orientation between socialism and capitalism defines the Cold War
as Jens's immediate frame of reference. The experience of other writer-
intellectuals could be adduced. In his book of lectures entitled *Begleitumstände* (1986) Uwe Johnson describes in detail his conflict with the
official aesthetic culture of the DDR during the fifties, whose officials
plainly experienced Johnson's literary modernism as subversive. And in
our post-Cold War era, not much has changed. The continued relevance of Jens's commentary is confirmed, if any corroborating evidence
is needed, by the *fatwa* placed on Salman Rushdie by the theocratic
Iranian state.

For Jens as for Trilling, it is the task of literature and the civic duty
of the critic to undermine the certainties, the platitudes, the nostrums
of an oppressive status quo. Among the liberal-minded intelligentsia of
German letters, this meant not only opposition to Soviet policy in the
East bloc but primarily opposition to the conservative restoration under way during the administration of Adenauer and his successors.

Significantly, in his classic 1957 study of modernism, *Statt einer
Literaturgeschichte* (Instead of a Literary History), Jens turns his attention especially to Kafka's persona, giving it more emphasis than his
fiction. He pictures Kafka as an "Ahasuerian outcast" driven by deep
religious need. In so saying, Jens does not align himself with Brod's
image of Kafka as a modern saint seeking to redeem the soul of modernity. By the fifties Brod's views had not disappeared, but they had
been widely criticized and were discredited in the eyes of most Kafka
critics (Heller 1952). What Jens has in mind instead is a strategy of
legitimating and thereby containing the illiberal element that is prominent in the work of many modernists but especially in that of Kafka.

As a trained classicist, a passionate advocate of republican democracy, and a believing Christian living after the moral catastrophe of National Socialism, Jens must have felt a considerable religious need of his
own. The overall plan of *Statt einer Literaturgeschichte* is conceived so
as to show that modernism revives and revises biblical and ancient
Greek myth. Modernism, including German modernism, is supposed
to be significantly continuous with our deepest roots in classical and
Hebrew antiquity. Thus restoration of the German tradition's embeddedness in the Western tradition is the book's basic impulse.

James Joyce's *Ulysses* is for obvious reasons the book's centerpiece, and Kafka, also for obvious reasons, presented something of a problem. Since Kafka plainly rejects the tradition of classical myth in his ironic retellings (for example, "Prometheus" and "Das Schweigen der Sirenen"), and since the Job-like character of Josef K. in *Der Proceß* cannot persuasively be read as an affirmation of the biblical tradition, Jens sought confirmation for his thesis in Kafka's biography and identity. This is what compels him to take up the Wandering Jew motif, calling attention to Kafka's critique of the cultural inauthenticity of assimilated Jewry and his nostalgia for the supposedly greater authenticity of Eastern European Jewry.

Jens cites a letter that relates the story of a trip Kafka took with Georg Langer, a friend who, unlike Kafka, later took the leap into Hasidism. The two were staying at a health resort in which a charismatic rebbe from Belz was holding court. Jens lingers over Kafka's admiring description of the exotic rabbi, but then he leaves out the part of the letter in which Kafka makes fun of the cult figure and his devoted followers. All his life Kafka was unable to reconcile his romantic yearning for membership in a mythic community with his unimpeachably critical, demystifying intelligence. Instead of facing Kafka's corrosive skepticism head-on, Jens shifts the terms of debate onto his own ground. That ground is the reconciliation of the new and the modernist with the ancient and traditional. Seeking forms of reconciliation in Kafka, Jens imputes to him a wish for the reconciliation between Eastern and Western Jewry, the modern secular Jew and the premodern religious Jew. It replays in miniature the basic motif of his study, while at the same time sidestepping the necessity of coming to terms with the fiction of a writer in whose work reconciliation is not a prominent feature.

It should be remembered, too, that the Cold War in the Federal Republic was an era of conservative restoration. Intellectuals to the left of center witnessed with alarm the rearmament of the nation, the authoritarian habits of government under Adenauer and Erhard, its sluggishness and reluctance to pursue the Nazi war criminals within its own ranks, and even a major attack on the free press (the *Spiegel* affair of 1962–63). Not a few "subversive" writers and intellectuals knew themselves to be under surveillance.

Under these circumstances Jens and other literary minds of emphatically democratic, antiauthoritarian stamp responded by insisting on the transformative, liberating potential of the literary tradition. The cultural crisis of Jens's generation led him back to the traditionally

German assumption that order and harmony in the polity begin with "aesthetic education." For Jens in particular, the tradition of aesthetic education reaches beyond German classicism all the way back into classical and biblical antiquity. As one of Germany's exemplary public intellectuals, he threw the weight of all his considerable prestige and rhetorical eloquence behind the idea that the Western humanist tradition remains an integral and indispensable element of our political and moral well-being (1972). It is for this reason that Kafka must sit uneasily in the canon for Jens, as for Trilling. Kafka's skeptical sensibility is not easily enlisted on the side of political optimism and social progress.

The defining paradox of Kafka's reception during the Cold War in Germany, then, is this: he is made to belong to a tradition of aesthetic humanism that his fiction radically questions. His elevation into the canon occurred partly in opposition to the Nazi oppression that had banned him as a Jew and as a decadent, partly in opposition to the Soviet oppression that banned him as a bourgeois decadent, and partly as a critique of the Adenauer regime's authoritarian machinations. But if Kafka, simultaneously apolitical and subversive, can be called on to witness against National Socialism and the various species of Cold War oppression, can he also be pressed into service on behalf of liberal, enlightened views of freedom and democracy? How subversive is Kafka? What enlightened hermeneutic can contain the nihilism of his vision? Or is he actually a cultural conservative, as some of the student radicals of the late sixties claimed? This conflict is the one that burns beneath the surface of both public and academic Kafka criticism during the fifties and sixties.

Kafka as Continuator of German Classicism

The rehabilitation and canonization of Kafka in Germany during the fifties took place so quickly that it is not possible to isolate any single origin. While the members of Gruppe '47 were talking about Kafka in their colloquia and writings, university professors were busily publishing articles and books. Foremost among them was the eminent Berlin professor Wilhelm Emrich, whose massive *Franz Kafka* appeared in 1958. It and its companion volume, *Die Weltkritik von Franz Kafka*, which appeared simultaneously, constituted the first all-inclusive study of Kafka and his works to appear in any language. And though there is no reason to believe it had much impact outside the academic community, within that community it has been a benchmark in Kafka studies.

That Emrich held a prestigious academic chair in divided Berlin, the city most affected by political realities during the Cold War, may help account for his slightly eccentric stance as a West German critic of the fifties. Emrich's criticism did not share the ahistorical text-immanent approach of his formalist peers Emil Staiger and Wolfgang Kayser. It was geared more toward showing how a writer's work is morally integrated into the social and intellectual world. This is not to say that Emrich's criticism was openly political. With a few exceptions it was not (Emrich 1963a). Nevertheless, his strong advocacy of literary modernism discloses a liberal confidence in literature's critical, oppositional task in a free society (Emrich 1954 and 1956).

In his 1956 essay on literary revolution and modern society Emrich posits the theme that dominates his Kafka criticism and his understanding of the modernist "literary revolution" of which Kafka was the prime representative. It is the theme of the free and autonomous individual struggling to assert himself against the dehumanizing forces of modern society. Josef K.'s battle against the unseen court and K.'s duel with the castle are viewed through this lens, though it is colored more by a phenomenologically informed philosophical anthropology than the sense of political urgency that had driven Arendt's critique. Herein lies the main difficulty in Emrich's Kafka studies. The unstated, vague philosophical underpinnings of Emrich's argumentation vitiate and limit its power of explanation. Indeed, Emrich's argument is often hard to follow because he qualifies and modifies his assertions to such an extent — and usually in the direction of prolix abstraction — that it is sometimes hard to know where he stands.

Even without a rigorously defined framework, certain currents emerge as central. One is the idea that Kafka belongs in a tradition that reaches back into German classicism. Emrich begins his magnum opus of 1958, *Franz Kafka*, with the proposition that German classicism characteristically dwells on *das Allgemeine* while Kafka, the exemplary modernist, focuses his attention on *das Individuelle*. According to Emrich, Kafka thus complements and completes German classicism. It is a shrewd turn of argument designed to contain the potentially illiberal force of Kafka's skepticism. Through the figure of complementarity, Emrich is able to claim Kafka is both radically modern yet at the same time all of a piece with the tradition against which he has rebelled. With Kafka embedded in the tradition of liberal humanism,

K. will fall into place as a rebel against the forces of oppression, anonymous though they be.

The cornerstone of his argument about *Das Schloß* is K.'s supposed vocation. Surveying the land implies measuring anew, reassessing, and therefore possibly overthrowing the status quo. K.'s aim is to be understood, in this view, as a revolutionary act. But as many other commentators have pointed out, the German word for surveyor, *Landvermesser*, plays on the verb *vermessen* and its various forms, which offer a spectrum of connotations including not only audacity and mismeasure but also (contra Emrich) false pretentions. Indeed, K. may not be what he says he is. Gardena, for one, suspects he is a tailor or haberdasher. In any case, the village superintendent assures K. that no surveyor is needed, and he plainly has no fear of K. in that capacity. In general, the villagers seem uninterested in K.s activity, except when they are irritated because he is useless and frequently in the way, as he is while camping out with Frieda in the schoolhouse. Their annoyed indifference to him suggests that a political dimension is, if not absent, at least not primary.

K. himself says as much. When he learns that the local cobbler, Brunswick, once agitated unsuccessfully in the village to get some surveying done, K. speculates to himself that he might yet find a confederate. Otto Brunswick "war . . . doch, wenigstens nach dem Bericht des Gemeindevorstehers, der Führer derjenigen gewesen, welche, sei es auch aus politischen Gründen, die Berufung dieses Landvermessers verlangt hatten" (S 185). The subjunctive qualification, "even if only for political reasons," reveals that K.'s own intentions are unpolitical.

The rebellious K., then, is not a revolutionary in the usual sense. Still, Emrich makes much of the evident oppression of the villagers, arguing they hope unconsciously that K. will liberate them from an unfreedom they are too inarticulate even to grasp. A few do so consciously. Pepi daydreams about K. as a "liberator of maidens," while Olga and her brother Barnabas have concrete hopes that K. can improve their lot, though not by liberating them — which Emrich does not point out — so much as by improving their standing with the castle. Frieda alone has a clear and practical sense of freedom, of a world in which things could be other than castle-oriented and castle-dominated. She proposes that K. run away with her to Spain or to the south of France. But K., the supposed liberator, shows no sympathy for her feelings or the freedom she offers.

All these things militate against Emrich's central thesis that K. represents the free self, one that is continuous with the Kantian tradition of Enlightenment, holding fast to its autonomy amid the forces that surround and oppress. K.'s kind of freedom is not of the liberal, enlightened sort. The autonomous Kafkan self is not political, not familial, not given to wholesome sexual pleasure or social life of any sort. Kafka's autonomy is one that is driven to the outermost limits of atomization and alienation. In these exegetical straits Emrich finds himself forced to resort to allegory, which means setting aside K.'s concrete and particular human relations in *Das Schloß* (and his own claim that Kafka is a poet of the particular) while elevating to primary significance an obscure layer of supposed existential meanings.

For example, Klamm is said to personify a "trans-subjective power of love," the sphere or state K. enters through erotic experience, one that K. must overcome in order to pass upward to heightened levels of human existence. Apart from the implicit misogyny of the claim that women represent a lower form of existence the hero must transcend in order to achieve the higher life, and also apart from the simple fact that in Czech (which Kafka knew well) *klam* means "delusion," Emrich also fails to clarify the particularity of these upper reaches and exactly what kind of progress K. has made by the end of the fragment. In the end Emrich settles for the unsatisfying claim that in upsetting the ritual distribution of the paperwork at the Herrenhof, K. has achieved something of import. The contention has little power of persuasion. The whistling, foot-stomping, and bell-ringing that K. incites have no consequences, revolutionary or otherwise, for him or anyone else. Emrich's finding is compelled not by the text but by the *Systemzwang* of his premise that K. is a rebel bent on changing the status quo. K. is more obviously bent on helping himself, and the confusion he creates is accidental, the comic result of his ineptitude and bewilderment in a world he cannot understand.

The turn into allegorical abstraction sets Emrich and his reader on a tortuous path of exegetical complications, qualifications, contradictions, and speculations that finally bury Emrich's arguments under a landslide of proliferating detail. Emrich's failure — if so influential a book can be called a failure — stems in part from an assumption that underlies his interpretive practice. With his strong orientation toward the organic model of the literary artwork, Emrich strives for a reading of *Das Schloß* that can account for virtually all symbolic detail. He treats *Das Schloß*, indeed all of Kafka's oeuvre, much as he had treated Goethe in his monumental study *Die Symbolik im "Faust II"* (1957). But even in Goethe, who wrote with the symbol stalker in mind, much escapes the system. And Kafka, who actively intended to thwart conventional interpretation, portrays a world in which the system, the whole, no longer exists. *Das Schloß*, an unfinished fragment, embodies the brokenness of the system.

This last point has become familiar in the postmodernists' inventory of themes, but it originated with Nietzsche: *das Ganze ist kein Ganzes mehr.* Hence it was an assumption that was also available to Emrich. But Emrich proceeds as if wholeness and totality had never been seriously put into question. From the contemporary perspective, it seems that totality, which Kafka resisted even in his completed works, should have been a rather more dubious category in Germany during the fifties. The example of Hitler's "totale Mobilmachung," the horrific results of "total war," the penetration of Nazi ideology into all aspects of public and even private life, along with Hitler's pernicious conception of the state as a total work of art, made the classical ideal of wholeness seem suspect, if not to Emrich, then at least to his contemporary in Frankfurt, Theodor Adorno.

Adorno's Kafka essay of 1953 reflects profoundly on the relationship between history, society, and the aesthetic fragment as form. By treating Kafka's works individually and collectively as an organic whole, Emrich undertook a 'total' reading that undercuts his own basic motive. He presents Kafka as a modern master aligned morally with the pre-Nazi tradition of German classicism. In Emrich's vision of literary restoration, the German classics, and especially Kafka, are meant to stand as a bulwark against the totalizing, totalitarian forces of the immediate German past, first of all, but also as critique of the communist repression that Emrich, as a citizen of Berlin, witnessed at uncomfortably close range. While offering Kafka as the ultimate nonconformist, he simultaneously claims that Kafka conforms to the classic tradition of German letters. Translated into the terminology of the Cold War, Emrich celebrates the subversive aspects of Kafka's fiction, yet he also finds it necessary to contain its corrosive power. Kafka's profoundly skeptical irony is difficult to control, threatening at every moment to subvert Emrich's own position.

Emrich's eagerness to fit Kafka into the classical tradition is rooted in the historical moment of restoration in Adenauer's Germany. German intellectual life, not least of all among academic Germanists, had been badly compromised during the Hitler years. In order to regain national and international respectability in the West, it was necessary to establish a new anti-Nazi, anticommunist literary canon. The harshest critique of the self-reconstruction of Germanistik came from the cultural critic Günther Anders. Since the early thirties Anders had been both a keen critic of Kafka's fiction (albeit a somewhat reluctant one) and a critic of the illiberal ramifications of his popularity in France and the United States, a phenomenon he referred to as the "Kafka plague." Speaking of postwar West Germany (and Austria) in a reminiscence on his Kafka essay of the late forties, Anders complains that Kafka was used to dispense a phony form of absolution:

> The idolization of Kafka dissolved the fact that millions of his kinsmen had been murdered. And if they made him famous, then not primarily as a writer, but as the man who delivered to them Josef K., a figure who, though *not guilty* was *punished anyway*. Of course I did not mean that the Kafka plague broke out among those who were unambiguously guilty and raged most ferociously among them . . . . Rather, the disease infected those Germans who were the half-hearted accomplices and who wanted to prove, also to themselves, that they could accept the guilt imposed on them by the victors at least in the form of literature. Remorse could be worked off in the form of art appreciation. (1984: xxxix)

Anders's critique is bitterly sharp and lacks nuance, but it stands as an acute, if partial, explanation for the process of Kafka's rise into the West German canon. In the DDR, of course, another mechanism for the repression of the Holocaust was already in place: the claim that the DDR was continuous with the communist resistance to Nazism. By proclaiming itself free of anti-Semitism and all other forms of continuity with the Nazi regime, the official culture of East Germany felt itself cleansed of guilt for the Holocaust and therefore uncalled upon to atone aesthetically or otherwise. Kafka was being treated there as a figure symptomatic of capitalist decadence.

Emrich responded polemically to the communist denigration of Kafka's canonical status. After having established Kafka's credentials as a link in the great chain of German classicism, Emrich continued throughout the sixties to promote his view that K. is a rebel-hero symbolic of the struggle against both fascism and communism. His anticommunist essay of 1963, a radio broadcast entitled "Franz Kafka between East and West," celebrates *Das Schloß* as an antitotalitarian masterpiece of German fiction (1963b). K. returns as the familiar rebel-hero, symbolic of the nonconformist, subversive values that West German liberals envisioned as their country's ideological future. But in this essay, K. is joined by Amalia, to whom Emrich imputes a similarly affirmative status because she rebuffs the sexual proposition of Sortini, a castle dignitary.

According to Emrich, Amalia's goal is the same as K.'s — rebellion. Standing eyeball to eyeball with the truth, she manages to free herself of the village's conformist mentality:

> Amalia bursts the social bonds to which her fellow villagers have succumbed . . . . And the villagers themselves — this is the decisive point — respect her decision. Indeed, they sense, even if only dimly, that only by means of a gaze like hers that reaches to the foundations of truth can a true, humane society be created.

It is difficult to see why Emrich thinks that Amalia is a respected figure. Frieda and the others openly despise her and her family. They are the village pariahs. As for K. himself,

> he wants a society of free, self-aware individuals who, in their "struggle" for autonomy also at the same time "survey the land" upon which all live and work for themselves and for society as a whole. Kafka's critical realism is therefore also a critically realistic humanism.

The Cold War imperative behind Emrich's remarks is plain. K. is made to sound like a smoldering rebel against injustice, the great-grandson of Götz von Berlichingen come to claim the family castle. Amalia sounds like an Amelia Galotti with steel in her spine. But in his zeal to recover a positive meaning from the pessimistic gloom of *Das Schloß*, Emrich fails to attend properly to the text.

The freedom of which K. and Amalia partake is a dark and empty one. In K.'s case, Kafka is explicit about this at the end of chapter eight. It is the scene in which K. waits alone in Klamm's coach because his scheme to waylay the elusive official has come to nothing:

> da schien es K. als habe man nun alle Verbindung mit ihm abgebrochen und als sei er nun freilich freier als jemals und könne hier auf dem ihm sonst verbotenen Ort warten solange er wolle und habe sich diese Freiheit erkämpft wie kaum ein anderer es könnte und niemand dürfe ihn anrühren oder vertreiben, ja kaum ansprechen, aber — diese Überzeugung war zumindest ebenso stark — als gäbe es gleichzeitig nichts Sinnloseres, nichts Verzweifelteres als diese Freiheit, dieses Warten, diese Unverletzlichkeit. (S 133)

> [It seemed to K. as if all connection to him had been broken off and as if he were now more free than ever before and could wait as long as he wanted here at this place that before had been forbidden to him and as if he had fought and won this freedom as hardly anyone else could have and no one could touch him or drive him away, indeed, hardly even speak to him, but — and this conviction was at least as strong —

it seemed at the same time as if there were nothing so meaningless, so
full of despair, as this freedom, this waiting, this inviolability.]

It is a moment of clearsighted self-knowledge from which K. learns
nothing and the reader learns much. K.'s poor freedom is negative, a
freedom *from* rather than *to* or *for* or *in* something. It is mainly a destructive emancipation from human responsibility. His shabby treatment of the loyal and trusting Frieda and his evident fear of being tied
to her suggest the destructive nature of his will to freedom. We should
remember, too, that he claims already to have abandoned the wife and
child in his native village, presumably also in the interest of his
"freedom."

Amalia's situation is more complex but little better. In her revolt
against Sortini's disgusting advances she displays admirable nerve. And
in the face of her family's calamity she remains loyal to them, in spite
of the fact that it was they, not she, who caused the family to be ostra-
cized by the village. It is she who cares for her decrepit parents while
Olga and Barnabas persist in their futile and, in Olga's case, debased
efforts to curry favor with the castle. Amalia, whose cold eyes and clear
vision are made much of in the text, has seen deeply into her situation.
She has risen above it by dint of her moral imagination. She seems able
at least to imagine a world in which the whims of castle officialdom do
not dominate the individual's life. Her retreat into silence is a step out
of the life in which all people talk and think about is their relationship
to the castle. She refuses to engage in the conniving and maneuvering,
the trading in castle gossip, which she calls "Schloßgeschichten," that
goes on all around her. So within the severe limitations of her situation
she has attained a symbolic freedom of sorts, while K. remains a slave
to the ethos of domination that he has in common with the castle.

Amalia's freedom in captivity remains a far cry from the liberal humanism that Emrich claims should emerge from our reading of *Das
Schloß*: "Without empty piety Kafka has translated and poetically renewed the classical legacy of German humanism that he adored and
honored throughout his life." What Emrich fails to come to terms with
is the bottomless pessimism of *Das Schloß*, pessimism about human
nature (as it is reflected in K.'s devious opportunism) and human possibilities within society (as it is reflected in Amalia's undeserved imprisonment and ostracism).

Exile in America

Inside and outside of Germany, Emrich's Kafka studies stood as a major point of orientation, but they did not alone dominate the field. In the sixties Walter Sokel, an Austrian-born American professor of German literature, rejected the prevailing wisdom of the fifties view of K. The consensus that K.'s duel with the castle was the revolt of a rebel against an oppressive counterworld gradually faded in favor of a psychologized version. The focus of attention of Sokel's massive book *Franz Kafka: Tragik und Ironie* (1964), and in general in the United States, shifts from the rebellious self in its stand against society to the anxious self locked out of society. Freudian criticism of an apolitical cast dominated American Kafka criticism of the late fifties, and continued until about 1970, when questions of language and form came to dominate and then cultural critique.

Sokel's exegeses offer the exemplary case for the psychological view. His K. is not so much a rebel as a fraud, and the novel's basic theme is K.'s attempt to make everyone, including the reader, believe that justice is the problem and that the injustice inflicted upon him is his motive in his struggle with the castle. One of the few things we can know for certain is that K. is a liar. He claims to have left behind a wife and child. He also says he is going to marry Frieda. He has to be lying about one or the other, unless he is a remorseless bigamist. Sokel somewhat arbitrarily decides that K. is lying about the wife and child, arguing that it is a part of K.'s need to invent a past for himself.

Sokel is certainly right that K.'s claim to be a surveyor summoned by the castle is untrustworthy. But it undermines the novel's fundamental hovering between possibilities to posit as fact the idea that K. is an impostor. Kafka makes it look as if K. is a phony: he arrives with no equipment (his assistants, he claims, will bring it); he never demonstrates any knowledge of surveying (but he is never required to); the assistants he claims are on the way never arrive (Artur and Jeramias come from the castle); the castle never officially acknowledges him as a surveyor (but it never says it did or did not summon him). Sokel works against his own persuasive emphasis on Kafka's cunning ambiguity by deciding that K. is an impostor.

Despite the case against him, Sokel's K. does not remain a negative figure. Like Emrich before him, whose work he frequently cites with approval, Sokel presses Kafka in the direction of traditional humanism, away from the emptiness, futility, and sense of nullity that pervade the book. Near the end of the castle fragment, argues Sokel, K. undergoes a striking moral transformation that elevates him to the stature of tragic hero (1964:462). Pepi catalyzes this improbable metamorphosis. Resentful and bitter about Frieda's social privilege, Pepi despises Frieda and tries to belittle her in K.'s eyes. K., who has just lost Frieda because of his manipulative scheming, defends her to Pepi. For Sokel, Frieda becomes the embodiment of higher moral values, and K.'s new self-knowledge is tragic.

The category of tragedy is completely out of place. The need to contain Kafka's subversive nihilism motivates Sokel's exaggerated insistence on a "tragic" denouement for the novel. Of course it is true that K. knows he was at fault for his break-up with Frieda, but he gives no indication that the insight means much to him, and he certainly shows nothing along the order of the pathos that goes with tragic remorse. The scene of K.'s transformation, the chat with Pepi, does not have much in common with Lear raging in the tempest or Othello's horrible moment of self-knowledge. Like modern people in a world in which "the tragic" has disappeared (even though misfortune and misery have not), K. takes these setbacks in stride. He inhabits a world without tragic insight. In fact, he is explicit about it. He tells Pepi that even if he had it all to do over again, he would behave the second time just as he did the first. K.'s one and only driving ambition remains what it was. He wants into the castle.

Apart from the misplaced emphasis on the tragic, Sokel's explanation for Kafka's overall intention as a writer is both appealing and revealing. It is ontological with an Sartrean cast, having to do with the modern individual's universal need to generate an identity from nothing. K., the fraud, must become the fiction he has created of himself. The novel "describes the fundamental situation of modern man, for whom neither the world nor his own self is given and certain" (1966:42). Sokel's case for understanding *Das Schloß* this way rings true. Still, lofty pronouncements also have their limitations. They supply a handy category for filing away a troublesome case, but they account for little of the novel's exact place in the larger scheme of things. Sokel's view takes for granted the sense of urgency, of felt actuality that the novel generates in its readers without exploring or defining what realities these features might be connected to.

Sokel senses this, as is evident in his occasional forays into literary history and sociology. He veers at intervals in his book toward the social and historical connections that present themselves. For example, he likens the world of castle and village to the microcosms of nineteenth-century fiction, Dickens's London or Balzac's Paris (1964:397); but, also characteristically, he refuses in principle to develop fully the connection he has invoked. His analysis remains a prisoner of the straitjacket of Freudian ego psychology into which he has laced it. Indeed, he explicitly warns against seeking larger and deeper connections, assuring his readers "that *Das Schloß* nevertheless remains true to the wellspring of Kafka's writing, i.e. to the dreamily alienated hieroglyphics of special 'symbols'" (Sokel 1964:397–98). The meaning of Kafka's fiction, according to Sokel's model of interpretation, is mainly personal and private. Missing are the specific social tendencies, the historical, human configurations beyond Kafka's immediate psychobiography that would give the account of Kafka's experience a better purchase on common reality. The hermeneutic circle here is a vicious one. Biography explains the text, and the text clarifies biography.

There is in Sokel's discussion of *Das Schloß* and Kafka's other works a strong presence of aesthetic autonomy in the sense given the term by the New Critics. The artwork presents a self-sufficient, self-enclosed world. Sokel breaks the spell, a least a bit, by insisting on the psychoanalytic link to the author's life. But otherwise Kafka's writing forfeits almost all other claims on the world outside the text. But the critic's situation — that it, Sokel's — is accessible to Freudian critique, though not in a way that was typical for critics of the late fifties and early sixties. The method of Sokel's analysis represses the social and cultural critique that inheres in the very structure not only of *Das Schloß* but in the novel as such, denying to it the direct and critical connection to the shared reality that is its legacy.

The novel, as a genre, is a public space. We know from Kafka's letters and diaries that he read his way deeply into the tradition of the novel. Kafka knew the novel's history, its possibilities, its many forms. That he did not finish or publish *Das Schloß* does not reduce it to personal and private self-expression. The very fact that he was writing a novel, even one not intended for public consumption, automatically places the book into a realm that is more than personal and private. He would have imagined readers, an implied audience that is built into the very idea of the novel. And the idea of the novel as Kafka knew it stood as a public space in which a story challenges and engages the critical faculties of its audience. He leaves to his reader the task of interpreting the conflicts he represents. It would be a strange and impoverished novel that excluded from its view any connection with society and culture, history and politics.

What makes *Das Schloß* especially difficult is Kafka's radical approach to the novel's traditional irony. This species of irony has much in common with ambiguity and undecidability and could also be called moral impartiality (but not moral indifference). Milan Kundera, an acute observer of Kafka's writing, offers a working definition of irony that is useful:

> IRONY. Which is right and which is wrong? Is Emma Bovary intolerable? Or brave and touching? And what about Werther? Is he sensitive and noble? Or an aggressive sentimentalist, infatuated with himself? The more attentively we read a novel, the more impossible the answer, because the novel is, by definition, the ironic art: its "truth" is concealed, undeclared, undeclarable. "Remember, Razumov, that women, children and revolutionists hate irony, which is the negation of all saving instincts, of all faith, of all devotion, of all action," says a Russian woman revolutionary in Joseph Conrad's *Under Western Eyes*. Irony irritates. Not because it mocks or attacks but because it denies us our certainties by unmasking the world as ambiguity. (1987:134)

The reduction of *Das Schloß* to psychobiography offers a reassuring feeling of certainty where there is none. It is achieved by renouncing the more uncertain task of engaging the novel in accordance with its traditional claim to a critical grasp of the world that the novelist shares with his or her readers. If Kafka's fiction continues to speak to an audience after he and his world are gone, then his fiction must have something to say *about* the contemporary world, too.

Work-immanent interpretation of the fifties and sixties proceeded at the cost of repression. What was being repressed specifically — not, I think, by Sokel personally, but by the institutional framework within which he was teaching and writing — was the reality of life in the Cold War atmosphere in which he and his readership in Adenauer's Germany moved and thought.[1] Political and social issues were automatically suspect, perhaps especially when raised by a critic who was an outsider. The émigré intellectual Sokel, as an Austrian and a Jew in the conservative (and sometimes anti-Semitic) setting of the American academy in the fifties, would have had little incentive to renew a tradition of cultural criticism that had been practiced mainly by the left-

---

[1] Sokel was living in the United States but writing in German, orienting his scholarship mainly to the German-speaking critics but also offering them something new. From the perspective of German academia, *Franz Kafka — Tragik und Ironie* was a fresh departure insofar as any sort of Freudian argumentation in literary criticism was still suspect there (Emrich 1965:110–12).

wing intelligentsia. One of the popular paranoias of the 1950s, as the Rosenberg trial showed, was the suspicion that intellectual Jews were likely to hold "un-American" sympathies with the left.

Seen from this perspective, Sokel's practical criticism becomes comparable to Lionel Trilling's later criticism. Both leave aside social and political issues in order to concentrate on the self as an autonomous literary value. Walter Sokel was a professor of German literature at Columbia University when he wrote his Kafka book, and in its acknowledgments he singles out Trilling for special thanks. The trajectory of Trilling's career in public critical writing ran from leftist social and political engagement in the thirties and forties toward a staunchly anticommunist liberalism in the fifties and sixties that stood aloof from direct engagement. The political transformation brought with it a literary critical withdrawal into the theme of 'the self' as a bastion against the increasingly ambiguous and embattled meaning of liberal culture during the Cold War. (Small wonder that Das Schloß, which explores the bewildering ambiguities of both self and society, was a key text in this atmosphere.) On a personal level, caught between the neoconservative reaction against the old left and the vulgar rowdiness of the radical new left (with its attendant hostility to the high culture he embodied), old-style gentleman liberals like Trilling were left out in the cold. The isolation of his position was reflected in his literary criticism, in which he increasingly sought a position beyond culture. He located this position in the autonomous self and the autonomous work of art.

In Sokel's presentation of Kafka's place in the era's culture we see a similar set of circumstances. Sokel's first book, *The Writer in Extremis* (1959), had been about German Expressionism, a topic that lends itself to social and political commentary. German Expressionists were frequently Marxists, activists, and radicals of various sorts, and Sokel explored these themes in detail. But there is also a line of Expressionist thought that leads inward. Significantly, it is this line that Sokel chose to follow in his Kafka book, leaving the other side of Expressionism behind, presumably because Kafka did not straightforwardly take society and politics as his themes. The question, of course, is whether the theme of private self drives out larger, more public concerns or whether they are somehow embedded in the problematics of selfhood. Sokel's version of the Kafkan self emphasizes the longing for detachment and "purity." The self seeks freedom from blame and responsibility by remaining aloof from the complexities of public life: marriage, work, family, politics. This is why Kafka's heroes are unmarried, disconnected loners.

Sokel does call attention to the social component of Kafka's fiction in one important way. He holds up the idea of *calling* as being particularly significant in Kafka's later fiction, not only for K., the would-be surveyor, but also for the hunger artist and the mouse-diva Josefine. Then he mystifies his own claim by suggesting that these fictional figures do not represent situatedness within a social category. Instead, they symbolize "pure ego," meaning one that is severed from worldly affairs, ascetic, and self-absorbed, one that alienates its bearer (or liberates him, depending on how you look at it) from messy involvement in society, including especially the grubbier details of sex and family life. In *Das Schloß* Amalia, who refuses Sortini's sexual advances, illustrates this principle.

The problem with this preoccupation with the "pure ego" is that it takes on the character of a worldview, becoming the single, all-encompassing principle of explanation. The immediate reference is to Kafka's well-attested longing for distance from sex and society, but the critic's own wish to remain aloof from the volatile issues of the moment are also reflected. The critic celebrates the pull back into the self and, though not completely detached from history and social life, has minimized its connectedness via an aesthetics of autonomy.

In the fifties Trilling had expressed reservations about Kafka's dubious meaning for the health of liberal culture. Sokel, writing a few years later — in New York, at Columbia, in contact with Trilling himself — dropped the issue entirely. Because Sokel was an advocate of Kafka and an intellectual associate of Trilling's, we might reasonably expect him to discuss Trilling's anxiety about Kafka's social and political meaning. His failure to do so, coupled with the fact that he largely sets aside any social and political engagement with the meaning of Kafka's work, suggests strongly that Sokel's criticism had already internalized Trilling's doubts about Kafka and the other modernists. By concentrating his analytic attention on pyschobiographcial explanations of the fiction, Sokel was acting to contain the darker significance of Kafka. *Das Schloß* and the rest of Kafka's subversive fiction is thus made safe for the liberal canon. Kafka's unpredictable and powerful critical energies are subdued, contained securely in the popular and harmless romantic tradition of the tortured, thwarted genius. For Sokel, the real story is not the one told in *Das Schloß* but the story of Kafka's life as a frustrated artist. That story is reflected in *Das Schloß* and elsewhere in Kafka's fiction. In the interest of telling the story of its author instead of its own, the novel is made to loosen its grip on social and historical reality and to become instead the symbolic working-through of Kafka's personal nightmares.

The nightmares are mainly oedipal. Sokel presents the castle novel as a punitive fantasy, linked thematically to *Das Urteil* and *Die Verwandlung*. It is personal inwardness made objective image through a literary process resembling dreamwork. In this Freudian dreamscape Klamm is the oedipal father figure; the power-hungry K. is in revolt against him, unaware that the castle is beneficent toward him; he struggles against Klamm for sexual possession of Frieda; the village teacher, Gisa, and other minor figures are agents of the paternal authority over the unruly son, enforcers of the son's banishment from the family; the assistants are his repressed instinctive nature. Via his Freudian analysis Sokel finally reaches a universal humanist existentialism. It is K.'s task to shape his own identity.

The reading is a reasonable one, given the parameters of its argument, but incomplete as it stands. It still needs explicit definition and historical specificity to justify the claim it makes. Freud fills this gap for Sokel. Referring the fiction back to the unifying, totalizing principle of a Freudian reading of Kafka's personal life, Sokel — or, to be fair, the discourse of academic criticism within which he was working — elaborately evades the larger task of interpretation.

The Cold War atmosphere sanctioned a literary criticism that did not meddle openly with matters of immediate relevance to the interplay of cultural and public life. In Kafka criticism the public theme of freedom gradually disappears, and the private theme of selfhood becomes primary. The emphasis on Kafka's riven selfhood, from this perspective, is oblique criticism of the postwar self. Sokel touches on this issue but never addresses it except in the most general way.

Still, there is, I think, more to Sokel's interpretation than meets the eye. Its historical grounding in the Cold War setting has been suppressed but can be recovered. Sokel's representation of K. as an outsider in search of an identity in a strange land also describes the specific situation of many émigré intellectuals in America. Forced by Nazi terror to flee Europe, most of them — like the two preeminent American Kafka scholars, Sokel and Politzer — were Jews in flight from the Holocaust. The fate they shared, prefigured in the experiences of K., must have helped to predispose people like Walter Sokel and Heinz Politzer toward Kafka and *Das Schloß*.

Austrian and German literary émigrés came to America and had to carve out a niche for themselves and, like Kafka's K., follow a calling in a place and at a time when German literature, to say the least, was not high on the agenda. "But we don't need a surveyor!" is a refrain in the novel that K. hears frequently. Beyond question, the struggle of Sokel and other immigrant German and Austrian literary intellectuals, most of them Jewish, in a new and strange country, where they had no past of their own, must find in K.'s struggle with the castle certain compelling points of resonance. Sokel has written that in Austria during the thirties Kafka had seemed boring to him. He discovered Kafka only after having emigrated from Vienna to New York, at a time when history had caught up with them both (Sokel 1991).

In his Kafka book Sokel departs from his exploration of Freudian symbolism long enough to argue compellingly that the castle's villagers show signs of traditional anti-Semitic prejudice in their treatment of K. (1964:414–15), though the emphasis falls not on the public aspect of the issue. Instead, Sokel lays it to Kafka's personal *"moi haïssable,"* as he discreetly puts it, finding self-hatred mirrored in the figure of K. The question of anti-Semitism in Kafka's life and imaginative work should be of the utmost relevance to any post-Holocaust understanding of him. It is a connection that is not only a part of Kafka's experience and reflection but must also have been fresh in Sokel's mind after his experience of Austria in the thirties. But instead of exploring the larger issue, which he raises himself, Sokel narrows his discussion to biography, offering Kafka's tortured love affair with the Catholic Czech Milena Jesenská and Kafka's anxieties about his Jewishness as an interpretation of the novel.

Sokel's discussion of the issue never opens to reflection about the bearing these matters might have on the novel as a critical piece of the public sphere *in the present*. Here is a truly subversive moment of *Das Schloß*, as Hannah Arendt had recognized. She includes Kafka and his K. in a tradition of writing that explores "the Jew as Pariah" in Western society (1944b). As she sees it, *Das Schloß* does not renew the myth of the "Eternal Jew." Its thrust is not mythic at all. It is a clear-eyed fictional probing of the theme of assimilation. K. is not portrayed as a Jew, of course, but the theme that Kafka explores in the book is one with special relevance for Jews. K. comes to village and castle as an unassimilated, unassimilable outsider in certain social and political and historical circumstances. K. is free, she argues, but his freedom is that of the outsider, the nobody.

Kafka exegetes of the fifties and sixties did not follow her powerful lead in the direction of cultural criticism. This was so perhaps because she herself did not follow up on her essay of 1944, partly because that early essay was misinformed in certain ways (she thought, for example, that Kafka was a practicing Zionist), but perhaps mainly because the topic offended an intellectual taboo of the era. The painful question of anti-Semitism and the awkward topic of Jewish assimilation remained safely, even doubly, contained by the prevailing discourse: first in Kafka's biography as the object of dispassionate and scholarly observation and second in the seeming remoteness of the pre-war Central Europe to which his fiction refers. The Cold War of the fifties was a time when Jews were at last finding their way into the upper reaches of the American academy. Lionel Trilling, Sokel's colleague at Columbia University, remains the prime example of the Jewish intellectual's successful assimilation into the American academy (Klingenstein 1991:137–98). In that climate, American anti-Semitism was a taboo topic in the discourse of literary criticism.

During the fifties and well into the sixties, the topic of Kafka and Judaism remained marginal to mainstream Kafka criticism. It was relegated to a secondary place under the rubric of biographical matters and to journals specializing in Judaica. Priorities were reversed. The issue of Jewishness was a matter of scholarly interest because it helped to shed light on Kafka. The more sensible view is that Kafka and his fiction have helped to shed light on diaspora Judaism and its special place in the history of this century. During the course of the seventies and eighties, the meaning of Kafka's Jewish themes emerged from the ghetto of special-interest journals into mainstream criticism, as Bluma Goldstein (1975), Marthe Robert (1979), and others have clarified both the specificity of Kafka's conflicted relationship to his Jewishness and its more general meaning for understanding Kafka's place in the wider context of literary modernism.

Since at least the mid-eighties, the centrality of these connections has become a matter of course for mainstream Kafka criticism. But in the earlier period they remain surprisingly understated. Even Heinz Politzer, who lived for a time during the Second World War in Palestine (as Martin Buber's secretary) and had written essays on Jewish and Zionist topics before, during, and immediately after the war, ignored the topic in his years as an American literary critic. He touches on it in his important study, *Franz Kafka: Parable and Paradox* (1962), but only insofar as it helps to explain Kafka's biography. He differs from Sokel in his more thoroughgoing skepticism about Kafka's self-presentation in the letters and diaries. According to Politzer, Kafka's writing, including his personal writing, was always imaginative and literary, never simply objective statement.

Politzer's main interest — and his compelling contribution to Kafka studies — lies in the area of narrative style. He opens his book with an exemplary reading of the Kafka parable "Gibs auf!" (Give it up!), meant to demonstrate the method that guides his reflections. The parable embodies what Politzer views as Kafka's all-encompassing strategy of ambiguity, which rests on the subtle and contradictory manipulation of narrative perspective. From this formalist standpoint Politzer argues persuasively against conventional interpretive modes anchored in historical, political, religious, and psychological models of understanding. The general thrust of his presentation is disarmingly simple: all paths of interpretation in Kafka's fiction lead to paradox. No univocal meaning or even basic consensus about his fiction can be reached: "All that Kafka wrested from the silence surrounding him was the insight 'that the incomprehensible is incomprehensible, and this we already knew'" (21).

In one way Politzer belongs to the Cold War trend of Kafka criticism. He withdraws from public cultural concerns into private, academically contained issues of textual autonomy. But to criticize Politzer this way would be reductive. He is right about Kafka and paradox. Kafka's narrative style is autonomous, and it does resist conventional interpretation. So even if Politzer's Kafka is partly a construction of Cold War aesthetics, there is another sense in which Politzer's departure from the era's conventions is striking. He accepts Kafka's nihilistic gloom as a comment about the world that is to be taken seriously, not interpreted away. More than any of his peers, Politzer accepts Kafka as genuinely subversive.

According to Politzer, Kafka's nihilism is not a moral flaw to be glossed over, denied, or exegetically bulldozed into an affirmation of humanist values. Politzer, perhaps bravely, considering the conformist intellectual climate — or maybe just stubbornly — lets Kafka stand. His *Schloß* commentary explores the art and background of Kafka's achievement without trying to salvage from it an optimistic, prodemocratic significance. Moreover, Politzer wrote in an urbane and accessible prose that did not sacrifice communication to the usually self-serving complexity of the professional academic. His book presumably reached a literary intelligentsia outside the university, and inside the university's reigning Kafka orthodoxy it struck a nerve.

The academic Kafka establishment recognized his powerful book as an assault on the sanitized, democratic classic they had constructed during the fifties. Academic reviewers either passed over the book in silence (it received remarkably few reviews) or, as in the case of Wilhelm Emrich, condemned it publicly in unusually aggressive terms. Emrich, who saw in Kafka a reprise of German classicism, fulminated against Politzer's "malicious," "primitive," and "naive" "misinterpretations." In fact, he was so exercised over the proposition that truth and the absolute may be inaccessible that he did not even stop short of denouncing his American colleague's views of Kafka as typically fascist (Emrich 1968:107). Politzer, of course, was a Jewish fugitive from German fascism and had come to the United States via Israel. Emrich's tirade, silly and insulting as it is, does at least help give a measure to the strong undertow that cultural politics exerted on Kafka criticism.

The View from the East

If Kafka was a thorny issue on the Western front of the Cold War, he proved even more problematic in the Eastern Bloc. His principal antagonist in the Soviet sphere of influence at the height of the Cold War was Georg Lukács. In 1955 Lukács gave a series of three lectures on modernist fiction at the Akademie der Künste in Berlin. Collected under the title *Wider den mißverstandenen Realismus* (1958; *Realism in Our Time*, 1962), they argued that "the dogmas of 'modernist' anti-realism" perversely glorify the emptiness and degradation that are at the center of bourgeois, capitalist society. Lukács's animus against Joyce, Beckett, Proust, Gide, Kafka and many others originates in the unhistorical concept of literature to which he came in his Stalinist (and post-Stalinist) period. Nineteenth-century realism, he claims in the lecture provocatively entitled "Franz Kafka oder Thomas Mann?" is not just one style among others but is the foundation of literature itself.

Modernist fiction — with its supposedly ahistorical emphasis on subjectivity, fragmentation, and nihilism — surrenders human dignity to the pathological anxieties of the late capitalist bourgeoisie. Kafka, who serves as Lukács's chief exhibit, will finally be rejected even though Lukács writes appreciatively of the "extraordinary immediacy and authenticity" of his prose fiction. Talent alone cannot save him from being cast into outer darkness in the odd company of Gottfried Benn and Ernst Jünger. Kafka falls short because his talent is directed inward, "substituting his *Angst*-ridden vision of the world for objective reality." Narrative technique cannot be enough if it is not guided by what Lukács calls the right perspective.

By "perspective" Lukács simply means having the ideologically correct outlook. Disregarding Kafka's use of irony and his wry sense of humor entirely, and refusing to allow questions of form to arise at all, Lukács offers K. and Josef K. as the epitomes of the modernist condition, embodiments of an era at the mercy of incomprehensible terrors. Dread is the Kafkan "perspective," and, though Lukács does not develop the point himself, he would no doubt have felt supported in his view by a deeper understanding of Kafka's finely nuanced manipulation of narrative point of view. Before continuing with the discussion of Lukács, it will be helpful to develop the relationship in Kafka between individual consciousness and narrative point of view.

In *Die Verwandlung, Der Proceß, Forschungen eines Hundes,* and many other works Kafka subtly exploits the resources of a peculiarly disembodied third-person narrative technique to lock his reader to the protagonist's perspective. It is a point that has special relevance to *Das Schloß.* The first forty-two pages of the castle manuscript were composed as a first-person narrative (making K. reminiscent, perhaps, of Robinson Crusoe finding his way in a strange world). However, at that point Kafka went back and changed the first-person point of view to the third and then continued writing from there in the third person. What Kafka gains by the extra bend in his narrative helix is an added dimension of uncertainty. We cannot know the precise limits of the narrative voice's reliability. No longer attached directly to a narrating *I,* the narrative voice hangs unsupported in abstract narrative space somewhere between subject and object. It cannot vouch for full insight into either. The voice is much closer to K. than to the castle world, yet the reader remains stranded in rhetorical space, simultaneously and paradoxically joined to and detached from K.'s consciousness.

If we cannot know *all* about K.'s mind, or even what the limits of our knowledge of it are, it is at least clear that we cannot know more than K. does about the castle and the village (except for what he may have expected, if anything, before he arrived). The reader's knowledge of what is going on is limited in varying degrees to what K. knows — or thinks he does. Take for example this passage early in the book:

> Nun sah er oben das Schloß deutlich umrissen in der klaren Luft und noch verdeutlicht durch den alle Formen nachbildenden, in dünner Schicht überall liegenden Schnee. Übrigens schien oben auf dem Berg viel weniger zu sein als hier im Dorf, wo sich K. nicht weniger mühsam vorwärtsbrachte als gestern auf der Landstraße. Hier reichte der Schnee bis zu den Fenstern der Hütten und lastete gleich wieder auf

dem niedrigen Dach [*sic*], aber oben auf dem Berg ragte alles frei und leicht empor, wenigstens schien es so von hier aus. (S 12–13)

[Now he saw the castle up above sharply outlined in the clear air. It was made clearer still by the light dusting of snow that emphasized all its contours. In addition there seemed to be much less snow up on the mountain than here in the village, where K.'s progress was no less laborious than it had been yesterday on the road. The snow here came up to the windows of the cottages and then also bore down again on the low rooftop. But on the mountain everything soared freely and weightlessly upward, or at least that is how it appeared from here.]

The crisp, hard-edged language of the passage reports K.'s visual perception as he looks up at the castle. It begins by describing what K. actually sees and then grades over almost imperceptibly into what he thinks about what he sees: up on the mountain everything rises upward "freely" and "weightlessly," as opposed to the things down in the village. Then Kafka even adds a blunt cue for his readers: "or at least that is how it appeared from here."

In the next paragraph objective visual impressions reveal more fully K.'s inner self or, to borrow Auerbach's famous phrase, "the contents of consciousness." K. interprets:

Im Ganzen entsprach das Schloß, wie es sich hier von der Ferne zeigte, K.'s Erwartungen. Es war weder eine alte Ritterburg, noch ein neuer Prunkbau, sondern eine ausgedehnte Anlage, die aus wenigen zweistökkigen, aber aus vielen eng aneinanderstehenden niedrigern Bauten bestand; hätte man nicht gewußt daß es ein Schloß ist, hätte man es für ein Städtchen halten können. Nur einen Turm sah K., ob er zu einem Wohngebäude oder einer Kirche gehörte war nicht zu erkennen. Schwärme von Krähen umkreisten ihn. (S 13)

[On the whole, the castle, as it showed itself in the distance, met K.'s expectations. It was neither an old chivalric fortress nor a modern mansion. Rather, it was an extended compound comprising a few two-story and a great many low buildings that were crowded together: had one not known it to be a castle, one would have taken it for a little town. K. saw but a single tower. Whether it belonged to a residence or to a church could not be ascertained. Swarms of crows were circling around it.]

Suspicion and conjecture, knowledge and ignorance are thus tied directly to a narrative technique that emphasizes subjectivity. A substantial critical literature has grown up around this aspect of Kafka's writing. Walser, Beißner and Kobs, Kudszus and Cohn — to name only the most prominent — have explored the formal intricacies of Kafka's narrative style in illuminating detail.

It is odd, though, that little effort has been made toward specifying the relationship of Kafka's narrative strategies of inwardness to the ones developed by the two other dominant figures of modernism, Joyce and Proust. In the wake of Samuel Beckett's influential essays about them, Joyce and Proust are generally credited as being the revolutionary writers who shifted the locus of reality from the outward, objective world to the inward, subjective, verbal model of it.

The interior monologue of *Ulysses* and the remembered world of *A la Recherche du temps perdu* draw attention to the highly verbal texture of consciousness at work in the minds of the protagonists. Reality is individual consciousness, and consciousness is largely language. Kafka comes closest to them in the chapter of *Das Schloß* in which K. accidently meets Bürgel while he is trying to keep his appointment with Erlanger. The language of narration follows K.'s consciousness as he gradually drifts into sleep and then into dream. The seam between waking consciousness and the altered consciousness of sleep is invisible in Kafka's narration.

There is in the basic unity of individual consciousness with narrative point of view a strong element of naturalism in its bias toward the authority of scientific knowledge, and especially of the empiricism of the turn of the century. The mind perceives the world by sense impression or memory and then represents it to itself (and to the reader) as language. It is reasonably clear that Kafka's narrative style was indebted to the psychophysics of his time, especially as espoused by Ernst Mach and Franz Brentano (Neesen 1972, Ryan 1991, Heidsieck 1994).

In 1903 and 1904 Kafka did some university coursework in empirical psychology, and from 1903 to 1905 he met more or less regularly with the Brentano Circle of intellectuals, who gathered at the Café Louvre in Prague. Between 1904 and 1914 he was often a guest in the salon of Berta Fanta, in whose home both Freudian pyschoanalysis and empirical psychology aroused discussion. Brentano in particular must have made an impression on Kafka's imagination. Brentano proposed that the world comes to the perceiving mind mediated and limited by an "inner perception," outside of which no second, independent vantage exists.

An affinity between Brentano's psychology and a narrative mode that systematically excludes any Archimedean point of verification is plain enough. But it does not offer much in the way of interpretive power. The radical aspect of Kafka's imaginative achievement along these lines, and the step that moves him beyond the linguistic naturalism of Proust and Joyce (or at least the Joyce before *Finnegans Wake*) has to do with yet another displacement of reality. The inward turn of modernism moves the real world from outer objectivity to inner self; the Kafkan turn displaces it from the self onto that which mediates between the outside and the inside: language. The result is not an emphasis on inwardness in Kafka, but the relentless disappearance of the self, a dissolving of it that occurs in the prose.

Leopold Bloom and Marcel evoke a powerful, even palpable sense of inner reality and felt life. That strong centeredness is given to the reader as richly textured poetic language. Joyce and Proust evolved highly individual narrative idioms that celebrate their protagonists' inner lives by endowing that inwardness with substantial voice and linguistic body. Kafka's achievement is the reverse. It is a language purged of class and ethnicity and, for the most part, of personal and local idiosyncrasy.[2] The narrator, K., and everyone else express themselves in an artificially neutral, frugal mode. The language of *Das Schloß* is so spare that the protagonist does not get a whole name to himself. We do not know how he looks. His personal history is almost a blank. The Kafkan self is reduced, like the hunger artist, to bare bones, endowed with a vulnerability that makes every moment seem precarious.

Moreover, Kafka moved consciousness out of the Cartesian center before Heidegger did. From the passage cited above, in which K. looks up at the castle and finds it as he "expected," the reader (or, more likely, in the case of Kafka's strangely affectless prose, the *re*reader) is surprised to learn that K. has expected anything. We have reason to believe that K. may be lying about being a surveyor (he is dressed shabbily and, like a hobo, has only a knapsack and walking stick with him, no surveying equipment), so we have little ground to suppose he could have expected anything more than a night's lodging at the inn. In any case, we now have an inkling of K.'s inner life, his expectations. The castle looks about as he thought it would: it is not a medieval fortress, not a palatial new edifice, but a dilapidated compound comprising a few two-story buildings and a lot of squat surrounding struc-

---

[2] Some few Bohemianisms remain. One wonders if Kafka used them self-consciously, knowing they would sound slightly quirky to speakers of standard German.

tures, all jammed together. There is a tower, but K. can't tell whether
it belongs to a church or residence.

The upshot of this description is plain to the rereader: there is no
castle up there. K. himself recognizes the incongruence between the
word "Schloß" and what he sees up on the hill, but it does not occur
to him that the lack of a match between word and thing may deserve
some thought. It is a typically Kafkan ploy to forestall and thereby ultimately magnify puzzlement by passing on to the next point, which is
seemingly more relevant. In this instance we move from K.'s implied
expectation to his disappointment. He is disappointed at the squalor of
the place:

> Die Augen auf das Schloß gerichtet, gieng K. weiter, nichts sonst küm-
> merte ihn. Aber im Näherkommen enttäuschte ihn das Schloß, es war
> doch nur ein recht elendes Städtchen, aus Dorfhäusern zusammen-
> getragen, ausgezeichnet nur dadurch, daß vielleicht alles aus Stein ge-
> baut war, aber der Anstrich war längst abgefallen, und der Stein schien
> abzubröckeln.

> [His eyes fastened on the castle, K. went on. He cared for nothing else.
> But as he came nearer, the castle disappointed him. It was nothing but
> a truly wretched little town, made up of village houses, distinguished
> only in that everything might be stonework. But the plaster had long
> since fallen away, and the stone appeared to be crumbling.]

Once again the visual merges with the inward as one of the rare moments of memory occurs — though only "briefly," as Kafka emphasizes:

> Flüchtig erinnerte sich K. an sein Heimatstädtchen, es stand diesem
> angeblichen Schlosse kaum nach, wäre es K. nur auf die Besichtigung
> angekommen, dann wäre es schade um die lange Wanderschaft gewe-
> sen und er hätte vernünftiger gehandelt, wieder einmal die alte Heimat
> zu besuchen, wo er schon so lange nicht gewesen war.

> [Briefly K. remembered his hometown. This alleged castle was hardly
> superior to it. If he had come only to have a good look at the castle,
> K.'s long wandering would have been a waste and he would have acted
> more reasonably in visiting his old home, where he had not been for so
> long.]

The moment is not exactly Proustian, but the fleeting glimpse into K.'s
past still is enough to redirect our attention to his inner life. We wonder at his reasons for coming, for now it is clear that he has come intentionally and that he has come a long way. The biblical word choice
"Wanderschaft" gives a special resonance to his thoughts, but that

resonance is immediately annulled by the commonsensical talk of "acting reasonably." He now goes on to compare the past with the present in suddenly vivid language that intermingles memory and visual perception with judgment and surmise:

> Und er verglich in Gedanken den Kirchturm der Heimat mit dem Turm dort oben. Jener Turm, bestimmt, ohne Zögern, geradenwegs nach oben sich verjüngend, breitdächig abschließend mit roten Ziegeln, ein irdisches Gebäude — was können wir anderes bauen? — aber mit höherem Ziel als das niedrige Häusergemenge und mit klarerem Ausdruck als ihn der trübe Werktag hat. Der Turm hier oben — es war der einzige sichtbare — , der Turm eines Wohnhauses wie sich jetzt zeigte, vielleicht des Hauptschlosses, war ein einförmiger Rundbau, zum Teil gnädig von Epheu verdeckt, mit kleinen Fenstern, die jetzt in der Sonne aufstrahlten — etwas Irrsinniges hatte das — und einem söllerartigen Abschluß, dessen Mauerzinnen unsicher, unregelmäßig, brüchig wie von ängstlicher oder nachlässiger Kinderhand gezeichnet sich in den blauen Himmel zackten. Es war wie wenn irgendein trübseliger Hausbewohner, der gerechter Weise im entlegensten Zimmer des Hauses sich hätte eingesperrt halten sollen, das Dach durchbrochen und sich erhoben hätte, um sich der Welt zu zeigen.

> [In his thoughts he compared the church tower of his hometown with the one above him. The former, rising with confidence, without hesitation, straight upward, becoming younger and finishing with broad roofs of red tile. An earthly building — what else can we build? — but with a loftier purpose than the low clutch of houses and with a clearer expression than the dreary workaday world. The tower up above — it was the only one visible — turned out now to be residential, perhaps the living quarters of the main castle. It was uniformly round, in part mercifully concealed by ivy and with small windows that now were glinting in the sun — this had something insane about it — and was surmounted by a garret-like top whose crenelated wall, unsure, irregular, fragile as if drawn by the fearful or careless hand of a child, jutted into the blue sky. It was as if some wretched occupant, who justifiably ought to have kept himself locked up in the most remote room of the house, had broken through the roof and risen up to show himself to the world.]

At this point in his observations K.'s concentration is broken by a raucous swarm of passing schoolchildren. The passage breaks off when K.'s all but opaque ruminations have reached a crescendo in the baffling simile of a roused giant, or so we must suppose, since he is big enough to break through the roof of the tower. The tower itself, we learn on K.'s closer inspection, does not belong to a church but to a residence; the light reflected in its little windows has something insane about it; ivy "mercifully" covers it.

Where conventional habits of reading would ordinarily lead us to expect narrative psychology, Kafka gives us instead autonomous imagery. Odd detail is heaped on odd detail, and K.'s view becomes increasingly subjective. And the more subjective it becomes, the more incomprehensible it becomes. The language not only dissolves the identity of the castle in ambiguity and contradiction; it also dissolves the identity of the subject thinking in a veritable swarm of highly individual and precise yet strangely unrevealing thoughts and impressions. Perhaps the giant who should have known enough to keep himself under lock and key is meant to suggest K.'s darker side bursting forth. Structurally it recalls the scene from *Der Proceß* in which Josef K. discovers the Whipper punishing the two warders, the realization of his secret wishes. Such scenes of momentarily released repression are ubiquitous in Kafka's fiction.

But rather than rushing to interpret the details, it probably makes better sense to interpret the general impression that the passage as a whole makes on its reader. We are left with a sense that all in this world, including K., is somehow diminished. The comparison of towers embodies the tendency of the imagery toward a world that is impoverished, pressed down from above. K. notes early on that the villagers' heads and faces seem squashed from above into a squinting grimace. Similarly, the buildings are mostly low and ramshackle, as if having been flattened out from above by some invisible weight. It is, we are likely to suspect, the weight of time or history that is made visible in the squashed appearance, peeling paint and broken-down state of these buildings that, in addition, show no sign of twentieth-century progress.

In the lines that follow we learn that K. has been standing by the village church, which is not a church after all but "really only" a chapel, and that the nearby village school is also a long, low building. It is a stunted world. The feeling grows that the sense of diminution, bewilderment, and senescence that the passage evokes characterizes not only the castle but also the self that imputes it to the castle.

In Kafka the language of the self is largely visual. Mute imagery replaces the more conventional narrative psychology of Proust or Joyce. After the Kafkan turn, words, like the sunlight reflected in the tower's puny windows, do not penetrate. They have something demented and disconnected about them. Neither the light nor the gaze nor the language of description suffices to pierce the opacity of the image. They are reflected back at the protagonist-observer, whose own interior is as opaque as the tower's.

Certain things are conspicuously absent, as K. himself is the first to note, when he contrasts the castle tower with the tower of his home village. The castle and tower offer no sense of symbolic liberation, no classical proportion, no hint of human warmth in their features. Particularly powerful is the simple image that lingers in the imagination most menacingly: crows (destructive, unpleasant, carrion-eating animals) wheeling around the castle's otherwise lifeless tower. The human characteristics associated with the tower in K.'s imagination suggest an imaginative projection of the self. The crows are perhaps an oblique intimation of language's relation to the self, circling the dilapidated, evidently empty tower: "Schwärme von Krähen umkreisten ihn." Black and full of portent, they circle but do not touch at the center. This image, along with the others, evokes the destructive work of time, the process of decay, and the burden of mortality. The paragraphs in which K. views the castle are shot through with intimations of the uncanny and the sublime.

Lukács protests against this ambiguous representation of the world. He demands solidity, clarity, and ideological simplicity. All such evocative details are in his view the fatal flaw of modernism. The foregoing long digression on Kafka and perspective has been offered to define the object of Georg Lukács's rebuke more exactly than Lukács did himself. For his purposes, discriminations of this sort are beside the point. From the perspective of his critique, it is enough to know that Kafka emphasizes the protagonist's individual consciousness, a narrative stunt accomplished at the cost of social reality. Preoccupation with subjectivity sacrifices the general to the particular. Techniques for limiting narrative perspective deform and ultimately disintegrate outward, objective reality. Modernism is the literature of atomization, for Lukács, of particular cases severed from universality, by which he understands the natural embeddedness of human experience in a collective.

The modernist bias toward particularity is the key element in Lukács's condemnation of its literary culture. In contradistinction to Emrich, he argues that Kafka symptomatically fails to unite the particular with the general: Kafka's "aim is to raise the individual detail in its immediate particularity (without generalizing its content) to the level of abstraction" (45). Detail in Kafka does not serve historical and objective clarity. He uses evocative detail to make the world opaque and abstract. This abstraction, then, subverts classical humanism, denies the possibility of continuing the tradition of European letters (that is, in and as socialism), and leads to nothing less than "the destruction of literature as such" (45).

The near hysteria of this last remark belongs to the pathology of Cold War rhetoric, a subliminal allusion to the fear of nuclear annihilation. Lukács shares with Western McCarthyites, whom he derides at intervals in *Wider den mißverstandenen Realismus*, the hyperbolical dread of creeping subversion by decadent forces, and he shares with them the need to contain those destructive forces before total annihilation can occur, by which he means the destruction of the humane experiment in communism that is the heir to European humanism. The invocation of "destruction," too, is a telling metaphor, transferred as it is from the sphere of Cold War political rhetoric onto literature. Lukács makes frequent references to the threat of nuclear destruction from the barbarians at the gate of the peace-loving Eastern bloc; the structure of his argument suggests that Kafka is the literary equivalent of a nuclear warhead.

In Lukács's version of modernism, its principle apologist is Adorno, who in 1949 had returned from his American exile to an adjunct post at the University of Frankfurt. He replied swiftly to Lukács with a blistering critique entitled "Erpreßte Versöhnung" (1958). Adorno reproaches Lukács first of all for capitulating to the Soviet intellectual orthodoxy but also for his undialectical, ahistorical hypostasis of nineteenth-century realism as a universal literary norm. For Adorno, history and social circumstance find expression above all in literary form. It is precisely this point to which Lukács is closed, condemning out of hand any concern with composition and style as decadent formalism. Against the schematic simplicity of Lukács's culturally affirmative social realism, Adorno insists on the dark virtue of modernism's complexity (176), meaning its formal complexity, but also and especially its characteristic irony at work on the level of both form and content.

In Cold War criticism, complexity is in itself an issue of considerable import. It is associated especially with Lionel Trilling, who has been criticized for seeking in it a refuge from literature's political meanings. It is supposedly a dodge to keep him from having to take a clear political stand. Complexity finds its way into the mainstream of Kafka criticism in the sixties via Politzer's paradox and Sokel's irony. Admiration for the virtue of modernist complexity, also known as difficulty, has been criticized as a strategy of domination, a way for academic mandarins to perpetuate their aura of superiority over the uninitiated many (Poirier 1987). No doubt there is something to this last point, but the exploitation of difficulty by some for their own advantage in no way discredits or diminishes the hold that books like *Das Schloß* have on the modern imagination.

Kafka is the writer in whom subtle complexity reigns supreme. This Kafka must remain an ideal proposition, though, because the process of criticism, canonization, and teaching exerts a powerful leveling, normalizing pressure. The judgment of professional commentators is an amalgam of dominant and dominating opinion in which repressions are inevitable. The Cold War Kafka, as I have been arguing, is one in which the themes of freedom and rebellion were privileged by critics who valued the almost political concept of subversion. And from the perspective of Lukács and most other publishing critics of the Soviet bloc, literary complexity itself was denounced as a decadent and subversive Western influence. Kafka's subversive nihilism was answered on both sides of the Berlin Wall with the impulse to contain the threat, either by interpreting it away, containing it in categories of individual psychology, or by condemning it as pathological.

4: The Return of Allegory

IN *FRANZ KAFKA: Parable and Paradox* (1962) Politzer programmatically thrust aside the usual procedures for uncovering hidden meanings. His sensible proposition — that such meanings in Kafka's fiction, if they exist at all, must remain hidden — did not leave him with nothing to say. Politzer's book offers a variety of penetrating observations about Kafka and his work. Not least interesting among them is his view that Kafka's style belongs to a tradition that is fundamentally different from the one described by Erich Auerbach in *Mimesis* (1953). In his first chapter, which contrasts Homer's *Odyssey* with Genesis, Auerbach focuses attention on the Hellenic tradition of Western realism that runs from the Greeks to the novelists of nineteenth- and twentieth-century realism and even modernism. The question of continuation in the Hebrew tradition is not addressed.

Politzer argues that Kafka's elliptical, parabolic style links him crucially to the other dominant strand of the Western tradition, that of the Hebrew Bible. Homer's realism rests on conventions of linear time, fate, individuality and local circumstance. Biblical narrative, by contrast, is "fraught with background," as Auerbach puts it, meaning that it proceeds by narrative strategies of omission, irony, and a sense of detached impersonality.

Unfortunately, Politzer does not develop his provocative insight into a full commentary. Speaking in a general way, he sees the Kafkan protagonist as a man who confronts "powers which seem to draw him back to his childhood and, further still, to the unfathomable recesses of the memory of his race. Since, however, time seems to be suspended with regard to everything Kafka wrote, his narratives also point forward to the future" (Politzer 1962:19). This passage, both surprising and compelling, sits uneasily in a book that otherwise asserts Kafka's incomprehensibility. Moreover, the phrasing suggests that biblical and Jewish foundations are the underlying ground of Kafka's art — which might then serve the would-be exegete as a secure point of interpretive orientation. But it also proposes that the feature of timelessness, the lack of a conventionally realistic location in time and space, imbues Kafka's prose with the aspect of future referentiality, of prolepsis.

Politzer does not give examples or explanations to clarify what he means, but at least one possibility leaps to mind. Many commentators, after the Nazi slaughter of Jews, Gypsies, and others became known, proclaimed Kafka to be a prophet of the bureaucratically managed factories of death, as Arendt called the death camps. The more tough-minded critics took a justifiably dim view of elevating Kafka from writer to biblical prophet, yet the connection is too important and too obvious to ignore. Günther Anders is characteristically succinct and clear on this point:

> We all know all about the "living rooms" that the death-camp officers set up for themselves with overstuffed chairs, gramophones, and night table lamps, with no more than a wall to separate them from the gas chamber installations. K.'s living room in the school gym of *The Castle* is not a whit more fantastic than the "formal parlors" of the death camps, which certainly seemed normal to the people who used them. The insanely displaced, overlapping milieus that Kafka carries out are in fact a description of the reality that the "sphere of duty" and the private "home sphere" in fact interlock in a single reality. (Anders 1947:122)

Anders goes no further than this in linking Kafka to the "final solution." He does not propose Kafka as a prophet of the Holocaust. Nor did Politzer, who was no less a skeptic than Anders, accept the mystification of Kafka as prophet.

Yet it is difficult for the informed reader of postwar letters to read *Das Schloß* and not think about the concentration camps, of lives under the control of all-powerful bureaucrats, of their powerless subjugation to these bureaucrats' incomprehensible laws and whims. History makes the link inevitable. Yet Kafka died before the Holocaust, knew nothing about it, did not predict it. But there is a way of sensibly talking about Kafka and the Holocaust. Many of the postwar novelists who have written substantial fiction about the Holocaust — Aharon Appelfeld, Jurek Becker, Danilo Kiš, Primo Levi, and others — have claimed Kafka as a precursor. His imaginative achievement shaped their vision. In this way Kafka's works do point toward the future, as Politzer suggested. In this modest sense Kafka's castle novel did anticipate the future or at least has helped to make it, now past, intelligible to us.

Without explicitly saying so, Politzer demolished the conventional code-cracking models of interpreting *Das Schloß* and other Kafka texts, and in so doing he opened the way for new possibilities of interpretation. He did not explore them himself, satisfying himself with the thought that the incomprehensible is incomprehensible, a phrase borrowed from "Von den Gleichnissen" (On Parables). Yet in effect, he showed that Kafka's fictions do not hold a hidden meaning the way a hatbox contains a hat. Rather, meaning in Kafka is not so much revealed as generated, contingent on the particular constellation of text, reader, and historical circumstance. Each makes a contribution toward the production of meaning. This contention is no longer radical, but it remains important in the present context to emphasize its immediate relevance, because it points toward the return of allegory as the dominant mode of Kafka criticism.

By 1952 at the latest, when Erich Heller published his withering assessment of allegorical *Das Schloß* readings, the leading Kafka critics had ceased to take allegory seriously as an interpretive mode. Allegory was understood to be a narrative design whereby Kafka cloaked reference to some established religious, philosophical, or other reductive framework in coded imagery. But Theodor Adorno, influenced by the richer, more complex understanding of allegory that his friend Walter Benjamin had developed, perceived in Kafka's writing an emphatically allegorical vision of the world. Indeed, Kafka himself authorizes such a view. "Aber unüberwindbar bleibt für mich der trockene Aufbau der ganzen Allegorie, die nichts ist als Allegorie, alles sagt, was zu sagen ist, nirgends ins Tiefere geht und ins Tiefere zieht" (F 596). Kafka's allegories have the ability to pull the reader "into the depths" that Adorno and Benjamin were eager to explore. Allegory is for them not the reconstruction of an objectively intended meaning but a hermeneutic process predicated on the reader's critical, imaginative input for the production of truth.

Adorno's central statement on Kafka, his 1953 *Neue Rundschau* essay entitled "Aufzeichnungen zu Kafka," begins with the insistence that Benjamin's version of allegory best illuminates Kafka's work.

> With good reason Benjamin defined allegory as parable. It expresses itself not in expression but its refusal thereof, by a disjuncture. Allegory is parable for which the key has been stolen . . . . Every sentence says 'Interpret me,' but none will allow it.

At bottom this is the same aporia that Politzer described. But it leads Adorno to a different and more productive interpretive strategy. Adorno steps back from the texts themselves, and the hatbox model of interpretation, in order to examine the meaning of Kafka as a cultural event that is historically and politically situated. He warns that Kafka's very success tends toward a betrayal of his deepest significance when that success leads to the distillation of universal truths from his texts.

The absence of complacent certainties is precisely the point in Kafka. Rather than extracting truths from Kafka, Adorno offers a variety of tentative perspectives — political, historical, theological, psychoanalytical, and philosophical — that illuminate diverse aspects of Kafka's critical purchase on the world. Instead of sustained argument, Adorno weaves together more or less related, mostly gnomic, insights. For example: "In place of human dignity, uppermost of bourgeois concepts, Kafka's writing wholesomely recalls to us our resemblance to animals." Adorno leaves it to his reader to think through and intellectually test such observations.

The scattering of remarks that Adorno makes on *Das Schloß* in his essay do not add up to a reading of the novel. But the overall motion of his thought suggests some fascinating possibilities. He sees in Kafka's "ciphers" the emblems of social unfreedom, which function allegorically in various ways. Gesture is one of the most striking. Following the trail of clues from Benjamin's Kafka essay, Adorno expands the scope of Benjamin's basic insight, taking whole scenes as frozen gestures (most notably the whipper episode of *Der Proceß*). He also calls attention to the presence of photographs, which reproduce, magnify, and preserve isolated moments in the stream of time. Adorno has in mind, among others, the photo that Gardena shows K. (S 124–25). Though crumpled and time-worn, it captures for her the moment when Klamm's love messenger came to her. The picture catches him suspended in midair. Castle couriers, it seems, are given to athletic high bounces. And it eternalizes for her a moment in her past (the supposed affair with Klamm over twenty years earlier) that she has failed to transcend. Of the various elements available to interpretation in the imagery — the gesture of the aerial leap, the idea of the photograph as the appropriation of a piece of time, and the sorry condition of the photograph itself — the latter is most relevant. The picture is, as Marthe Robert aptly called it, a caricature of eternity. It reveals the passage of time, giving the lie to what Gardena has chosen to see in it.

Adorno does not mention Benjamin's interest in baroque emblems as allegorical signs, but Gardena's attachment to her photo suggests an emblematic significance. Its place in the world of the castle is subtle but important. There is conspicuously little in Kafka's novel that belongs to the modern world. Only three signs of technological advancement stand out: Gardena's photograph, the telephone at the inn by the bridge, and electric lights. They alone show that the castle and its village belong to our century. All else is feudally primitive and may as well be medieval (except that the low profile of Catholicism also suggests the postreligious, scientific era). The conspicuous modernity of these objects, then, imposes emblematic significance on them.

They are fragments of the twentieth century: the photo suggests the bad infinity of mechanical repetition; the telephone, the triumph of mass communication since the 1880s, fails to connect K. to the castle; and the electric light may be equated with the false light in which K. always sees things. The danger of overinterpretation is omnipresent, of course, but the pitiful inadequacy of these characteristically modern conveniences to improve anybody's life in the novel is hard to overlook. The novel forces these items on us as objects of contemplation. Like Hamlet contemplating the skull of Yorick, we are left to ponder the telephone that doesn't work, at least not when K. uses it.

The allegorical decoding of opaque signs and images is for Adorno a specifically philosophical form of interpretation. It does not simply uncover a fixed meaning that lies buried in the text but instead throws a momentary light onto it from a certain angle at a certain time. So Adorno — writing as an enemy of Soviet communism and a critic of Western conformism and mass consumerism — also sees in *Das Schloß* the petrified gesture of his own particular moment in the Cold War era: of different kinds of unfreedom in both West and East, though for Adorno the emphasis falls mainly on the condition of life lived under the regime of "late capitalism."

In order to explore what Adorno's standpoint might mean for understanding *Das Schloß*, it is necessary to go beyond his few comments about the novel and try to see it in the light of his essay as a whole. His emphasis on time and history in Kafka is certainly an aspect that needs fuller exploration. The castle, too, is an emblem, a narrative icon of sorts from the realm of fairy tale and romance that is presented as the object of contemplation. The image of a ramshackle edifice, more town than castle, suggests the demystification of a motif best known from its idealized versions. Traditionally, the castle is a utopian goal toward which aspirations are drawn, the place in which the prince and princess will be wed and live happily ever after. K.'s otherwise unmotivated desire to gain entry into the castle may be no more than a residual element of old themes of romance and fairy tale.

Kafka's castle also suggests the emblematic "ruin" that played an important role in Benjamin's analysis of baroque sorrow-plays. On the baroque stage the broken wall and ruined palace stood for the ephemerality of life, its fallen condition in this world. Similarly, Kafka's castle seems to be an image that time and history have hollowed out. Neither feudal nor modern, it is stuck between worlds, presided over by an invisible, improbably named count and administered by an impossibly unwieldy army of mostly snoozing bureaucrats. The masters sleep a great deal, as Frieda points out (S 65). And Frieda, the demystified princess of fairy-tale extraction, has not found much of a prince in K. Even erotic love, traditionally presided over by the divine Aphrodite, is within the purview of Klamm, a faceless, portly, middle-aged bureaucrat who wears a black frock coat and a pince-nez while dozing over his beer. All too few Kafka critics have responded intellectually to the humor in Kafka's satirical figures, probably because we are required by the structure of the narrative to share K.'s humorless perspective. And K. is nothing if not a serious fellow. In his world even sex is business (for him and for Olga): a means to a business-like, calculated end. It is also a world in which the structure of time is strangely deformed. When K. asks Pepi how long it will be until spring, she dreamily repeats his question.

> "Bis zum Frühjahr?" wiederholte Pepi, "der Winter ist bei uns lang, ein sehr langer Winter und einförmig . . . . Nun, einmal kommt auch das Frühjahr und Sommer und es hat wohl auch seine Zeit, aber in der Erinnerung, jetzt, scheint Frühjahr und Sommer so kurz, als wären es nicht viel mehr als zwei Tage und selbst an diesen Tagen, auch durch den allerschönsten Tag fällt dann noch manchmal Schnee." (S 388–89)

> ["Until spring?" repeated Pepi, "our winter here is long, very long and monotonous . . . . Well, eventually spring and summer do arrive and there is time for that, but in memory, now, spring and summer seem so short that it is as if they were not much more than two days, and even on these days, even during the most beautiful day of all, sometimes snow still falls."]

Not only are the seasons hard. K. also has a good deal of trouble with the daily passage of time during the strangely shaped seven days of his stay. Just when it seems to him that time has all but ceased, it unexpectedly lurches forward with a sudden nightfall, for example; time passes, when it moves at all, by fits and starts. And with time congealed into an endless winter, the human spirit is made stolid, drowsy, and immobile, a condition rendered as image by the bed-bound Bürgel. Klamm is seen only while sleeping; as far as K. or the reader can tell, bureaucratic tasks seem to be undertaken only at night; and night is the time of day that dominates the novel.

Permanent winter, the allegorical season of death, suggests a historical, or even moral time frame. The European experience of the

First World War (for Kafka and his coevals) did not thaw into Czech independence (of which Kafka took little note) but deepened first into the hard times of the twenties and then (for those who survived Kafka) into the numbing misery of the Second World War. The ruins of war, the ruins of European history, the ruin of civilized moral standards — the image of Kafka's shabby castle attracts these allegorical meanings like a magnet attracts iron filings.

Adorno and the Cold War

Adorno had returned to Germany in 1949, the year in which the Cold War split the country into two opposed and armed visions. He was able to remain unclaimed by either side because he was a sharp critic of both sides: of totalitarianism in the Soviet sphere, and of conformist mass consumerism in the American. Western conservatives viewed him with suspicion, fearing the subversive aspects of his partly Marxian practice of cultural criticism. Eastern conservatives viewed him as a reactionary bourgeois critic, as one of their own gone bad. In fact he was neither. In the end, though, the radical students of the sixties, attracted to the subversive elements of his thought and his criticism of the Adenauer era, felt betrayed by him and by what Habermas has called his "strategy of hibernation."

Adorno died in 1969, shortly after an unpleasant and, for the aging mandarin, distressing lecture hall confrontation with radical leftists at the University of Frankfurt. He was speaking on aesthetic theory at a time when militant students wanted action, immediate social and political change. Kafka and Beckett, the two mainstays of Adorno's modern canon, had become suspect in the politicized atmosphere of the mid- and late sixties. Adorno was accused of being an ivory tower intellectual at a time that, for the students, cried out for direct engagement. The effect of this intellectual climate on Kafka criticism, and on literary criticism in general, was divisive. Formalist studies of Kafka flourished. The academic critics, aloof from the marching and street battles, pursued the nuances of Kafka's style in idyllic Tübingen (Beißner, Philippi, Kobs) and elsewhere.

Another reason that Adorno does not fit the pattern of Cold War Kafka criticism — a reason, that is, apart from his unaccommodating intellectual nature — was his experience in the original phase of Kafka reception. Adorno came to know Kafka's work in its original context, a fact he emphasizes. His Kafka expresses that hunger for wholeness so characteristic of Weimar intellectuals, which is why the predominant theme of his aesthetics and his Kafka criticism remains the redemptive potentiality of literature. Adorno sees the redemptive modalities of Kafka in its negativity, in Kafka's refusal to accept the world in its degraded condition, in his very willingness to portray it as degraded (Goetschel 1985).

In a moral epoch as hollow and debased as the twentieth century, Adorno saw no possibility for a traditional, positive religious, political, or social renewal. This is why his final book, *Ästhetische Theorie* (1970), turned its full attention to art and the imagination. Only art remained as a redemptive possibility, though not in the classical sense of contributing an affirmative, transformative vision of modern life. In the modern or, more specifically, modernist era, it had devolved upon art alone to unmask as false consciousness the myth of civility with which the educated classes flatter themselves. Adorno rejected as kitsch any "affirmative" artistic vision as delusion, at best, but more characteristically as manipulation by the market-driven culture industry in the West and as an ideologically manufactured, phony doctrine of socialist realism in the totalitarian East.

Driven into these straits, true art must retreat into negation: Kafka and Beckett, Schönberg and Berg. "Das Negative zu tun," wrote Kafka in 1917, "ist uns noch auferlegt, das Positive ist uns schon gegeben" (NS 2:119): the task of accomplishing the negative remains imposed upon us; the positive is already given. Affirmation too easily accommodates the status quo. Only negation implies all that remains undone. The element of patient if critical messianism that paradoxically inhabits Adorno's vision of a negative aesthetics stems from the inability of official culture fully to integrate Kafka's fiction into its affirmative vision of itself. Even with his canonical status in Western Europe and the United States, Kafka's work has resisted total absorption into the culture industry. This is because there can be no consensus about it. The work remains baffling and protean, disturbing and dark, comic and ruthless. These traits have the effect of carving out a negative space in postwar culture that has not, or at least not yet, been colonized by commodity culture or totalitarian politics. It is here that Adorno, the famous pessimist, cautiously stakes out a dialectically positive claim: "If Kafka's work knows hope, then it is more probably in its most severe moments rather than its milder ones: in the ability to withstand even the worst by transforming it into language" (Adorno 1977:266).

K.'s stubborn persistence in the face of the castle may be an example of what Adorno has in mind, though it seems likely that the best embodiment of it would be Amalia. It is she, not the scheming K., who lives utterly without illusion and assistance (Dowden 1990). The redemptive hope that clings to Adorno's view, then, lies in his perception of Kafka's fiction as a way of holding out against the forces of dehumanization and conformity for something better, something yet to come that he cannot name.

> Es ist keine Widerlegung der Vorahnung einer endgültigen Befreiung, wenn am nächsten Tag die Gefangenschaft noch unverändert bleibt oder gar sich verschärft oder selbst wenn ausdrücklich erklärt wird, daß sie niemals aufhören soll. Alles das kann vielmehr notwendige Voraussetzung der endgiltigen Befreiung sein. (T 848; January 10, 1920)

> [It is no refutation of the intimation of a final liberation if on the next day the captivity remains unchanged or is straitened or even if it is explicitly declared that it will never cease. Rather, all that can be the necessary precondition of the final liberation.]

During the course of the sixties, though, as university students became politically radical and literature took a sharp turn into political *engagement*, Kafka's negativity became suspect. The famous 1968 issue of the left-wing journal *Kursbuch* can be taken as an index to the prevailing spirit of the student movement's literary position. Hans Magnus Enzensberger and Karl Markus Michel declared the literature of masterpieces, of great canonical works, to be a dead relic of the bourgeois past. They abandoned the assumption, common to Trilling and Adorno, that progressive formal complexity in literature went hand in hand with progressive social and political thought. From their perspective, Kafka's *Das Schloß* would be compromised by the insidious appropriations of bourgeois culture just as much as Goethe or any other classic.

The reason for their hyperbolical (and short-lived) gesture was the perception that traditional literature, including the complex classic modernists, had lost any subversive power they may once have possessed. Of course there were some efforts to redescribe *Das Schloß* as consonant with the interests of West German radicalism. In a special issue of *Kürbiskern* devoted to the topic of literature and the "class war," Hans-Georg Pott delivers an apologia in defense of Kafka. It identifies the castle's invisible power structure with the invisible power of capitalism (Pott 1977). Adorno had made a similar point in his essay of 1953, momentarily succumbing to the impulse of filling in the blank of Kafka's most exegetically seductive image with an abstract meaning.

But Adorno also offers other perspectives, some of which complement and others of which compete with his contention that Kafka's work in general can be understood as a "cryptogram" of life under late capitalism.

K. as Bourgeois

The politically charged era of the late sixties, whose direct after effects lasted through the seventies, divided literary criticism between right and left. With the exception of extraterritorial intellectuals, especially Adorno, critics on the left identified Kafka as a "conservative" figure. The influence of Lukács and of the East German critics, hostile to Kafka, was no doubt important for any writers of dissertations and habilitations who felt drawn toward the left. However, at precisely the same moment, Kafka's star was rising in the Socialist Republic of Czechoslovakia and among leftist intellectuals in France.

A shift began in the summer of 1962. In a speech he made at a world "peace conference" held in Moscow, Jean-Paul Sartre forcefully advocated what he called the "demilitarization of culture" as a part of peaceful international competition. Arguing that Kafka's fiction had been exploited in the West as a critique of Eastern bloc bureaucracy, he called for the Soviet ban of Kafka to be lifted so that the Marxist perspective would be allowed to unfold in all its fullness:

> True cultural competition, in a word, resides in thrusting aside the obstacles to culture and then issuing a peaceful challenge to the other side: To whom does Kafka belong, to you or to us? — i.e., who understands him best? Who profits most from him? (1962:328)

Sartre's smug confidence in the superiority of Marxist literary criticism was a corollary to Khrushchev's much-publicized boast that the USSR would "bury" the West in international economic competition. But more controversially, he was urging Marxist critics to take possession of Kafka and claim him as their own.

Eastern bloc critics of a reformist stamp seized the opportunity to rehabilitate Kafka. In Czechoslovakia Eduard Goldstücker organized a Kafka conference in a castle called Liblice in commemoration of the writer's eightieth birthday. Goldstücker, a Germanist at the Czech Academy of Science, had been cultural attaché to Israel in the early fifties but was called back and imprisoned for life for supposedly being involved in a conspiracy against the communist government. Eventually he was released. Though a victim of official Czech paranoia,

Goldstücker remained a committed Marxist and so dedicated his conference to the project of reintroducing Kafka into the intellectual life of Czechoslovakia and the communist world of Eastern Europe.

In his contribution, Goldstücker focuses his attention on *Das Schloß*, directing his critique of it toward the view that K. is a revolutionary bent on liberating the proletarians of the village (1963:43). His strategy was simply to assimilate Emrich's basic thesis to the doctrine of Marxist orthodoxy. Others emphasized supposed elements of socialist realism, but they most importantly reached something of a consensus that the central feature of Kafka's fiction was alienation and that it ought to be applied as much to the workers' movement as to the capitalist West.

The results of the conference were far-reaching in Czechoslovakia. It turned out to be a major signpost pointing toward the general liberalization of intellectual life that led to the Prague Spring of 1968. In the short run it led directly to the republication of *Das Schloß* in 1963 (it had been out of print in Czech since the early forties, when the Nazis had destroyed the original publisher's stock), and it turned Kafka into a topic of public discussion (Sartre, Fischer, Goldstücker, Kundera 1965). Indeed, the course of events in Czechoslovakia suggests that Kafka's modernism and *Das Schloß* may well be as subversive as the most dogmatic Soviet ideologues of culture had feared. Once Kafka became a part of public intellectual life there, the meaning of his fiction slipped beyond the control of the guardians of official culture. In Czechoslovakia Kafka became a symbol of the writer's conscience and the need to oppose intellectual oppression (Bahr 1970).

Hardliners from East Germany remained bitterly hostile to Kafka and to Czech liberalization (Fischer 1966). A few days after Warsaw Pact troops invaded and occupied Prague in August 1968, Klaus Gysi, the minister of culture in East Germany, held a cultural-policy speech. In it he attacked the Liblice conference as the beginning of counterrevolutionary activity in the Eastern bloc. The ostensible occasion of his speech was the reopening of the National Theater in Weimar, but he used the setting as a platform to denounce Kafka as subversive and his Eastern bloc advocates as the agents and dupes of Western propaganda. In his attack he poses a cultural choice for his audience: the classical-humanist tradition of Goethe (he identifies Faust with the working class), or the capitalist depravity of Kafka. And he concludes by assuring his audience that the Soviet Union had liberated the Czech people in the nick of time. They were endangered both from the imminent threat of "imperialist intervention from outside" and "counterrevolutionary putsch from within" (Gysi 1968).

Gysi was right at least about Kafka's subversive meaning for Czech intellectuals. Naturally Kafka, as a Czech and citizen of Prague, would have a special meaning for people like Václav Havel, Josef Škvorecký, Ivan Klíma, and Milan Kundera, all of whom were writers involved in the attempt to liberalize life in communist Czechoslovakia during the sixties. If conservatives were eager to construct allegories of Western decadence in Kafka, those who opposed official aesthetic doctrine responded differently. They recognized in Kafka and *Das Schloß* signs of their own alienated existence in a socialist police state.

The link between Kafka and the police is important. What is conspicuously missing from the castle and its world is, precisely, the police. They are absent because they are everywhere — or almost everywhere — fully internalized. Amalia alone has not integrated the police into her conscience. The best example of this process of internalization is her story, which is Kafka's satire of social control. As Olga matter-of-factly points out to K., the punishment of Amalia and her family was not the direct result of Amalia's supposed transgression but the result of the family's subsequent obsession with guilt. The castle undertakes no action against them. Their own feelings of guilt spread like a contagion in the village and transform them into the object of general disgust.

Kafka is satirizing people's willingness not only to accept the status quo but also ruthlessly to produce and enforce it. This does not exactly make Kafka a prophet of the police state, but it does make him an acute observer of human nature and social experience. And it provides the most central point of reference for the Kafka-oriented writers of the Prague Spring. In their fiction, life in communist Czechoslovakia is one in which the police are omnipresent, infiltrating the population at large. It is a world in which not only paid servants of the secret police might denounce a citizen, but in which virtually anyone might: a wife or husband, and old friend, a lover, a trusted colleague. In Milan Kundera's hilariously sad first novel, *The Joke* (1965), Ludvik, a staunchly Marxist student, writes his girlfriend a postcard with some irreverent witticisms about communism. His mirthless lover turns the missive over to a student leader with even less sense of humor, who in turn passes the card on to the authorities. Ludvik is expelled from the party and the university and eventually lands in a labor camp. After the 1968 crackdown, Kundera himself lost his teaching position and saw his works removed from bookstores and libraries.

Kundera is a close student of Kafka, especially when it comes to relations of domination in sex and politics. According to him, the totalitarian state strives to abolish the boundary between public and private. It wants society to be one big family in which no one has any secrets. Total surveillance is its ideal. In consequence, Kundera rejects as a sentimentalism the common notion that K. is seeking to establish himself as a member of the community. In its place he offers the tough-minded, acutely critical view that K. is after something else altogether:

> The Land-Surveyor K. is not in the least pursuing people and their warmth, he is not trying to become a "man among men" like Sartre's Orestes; he wants acceptance not from a community but from an institution. To have it he must pay dearly: he must renounce his solitude. And this is his hell: he is never alone, the two assistants sent by the Castle follow him always. When he first makes love to Frieda, the two men are there, sitting on the café counter over the lovers, and from then on they are never absent from their bed. (1979:111)

In the castle's world, public and private interpenetrate each other almost completely. No police are needed because no one has any secrets. The police are present in each villager as surely as they are present in Ludvik's patriotic girlfriend.

Kundera's view is paradigmatic for the kind of allegorical insight into *Das Schloß* that, driven by cultural forces that are variable, produces viable meanings. There is no sovereign and separate meaning that is fully formed in advance of the reader's encounter with the work. Interpretation that is authentically philosophical, wrote Adorno in 1931, "does not home in on a meaning that lies ready and waiting behind the question. Rather, it illuminates the question with a sudden and momentary light that consumes it at the same time" (1973:335). Our text of *Das Schloß* is incomplete, possibly jumbled, and certainly contradictory; it does not contain within itself a pure, secret meaning just waiting — like the good prince within the frog (or beetle) — for the magic kiss of exegesis to restore it to its true form. However, the condition of contingency in interpretation does not rob *Das Schloß* of its meaning; indeed, it multiplies the possibilities for authentic interpretive encounters with the novel.

Academic critics of the sixties, mistrustful of the link between individual reading and larger cultural experience, continued the search for secure foundations upon which to build a permanent understanding of *Das Schloß*. In France it meant the turn away from the various existentialist readings of Kafka by Camus, Sartre, and Blanchot toward the seemingly scientific certainties of structuralist analysis. Camus's famous essay of 1942 had made Kafka into an exponent of Camus's own view of the cosmos as absurd. Sartre occasionally mentions Kafka in his works — always with great approval — but nowhere does he systematically explore *Das Schloß* or any of the other writings. Only Blanchot, who sought in Kafka a confirmation of his thoughts about the relationship of literature to death, wrote extensively on Kafka. Blanchot understood the opacity of *Das Schloß* to embody the pure autonomy of literature, its absolute separation from history and society. In his essay of 1964 "Le pont de bois" (The Wooden Bridge), Blanchot approaches *Das Schloß* via the problem of literary commentary.

The commentator, or interpreter, aims to resolve the tension between text and world by explaining how the two are linked. To do so she must fill in the missing pieces or, to put it more simply, spell out the castle's hidden meaning. But the opacity, according to Blanchot, is absolute. The missing pieces that would explain the novel are beyond all recovery. It is this condition of the novel's permanent incompleteness — both as unfinished fragment and as opaque aesthetic artifact — that make of *Das Schloß* a work of representative significance. It emphasizes the unbridgeable gap between text and world. This gap leaves it continually in want of a completion that commentary always tries to supply. Incompleteness, want, absence — what he calls *le neutre* — are the condition of literature itself, a state of affairs that Blanchot believes himself to have discovered in the castle: an image of the void that cannot be filled.

Blanchot's argument that *Das Schloß* stages the autonomy of art is a shrewd way of trying to avoid the various dead ends of allegorical interpretation, all of which attempt, unsatisfactorily, to fill the void with a meaning. But Blanchot has not escaped the aporia of allegories. He has turned *Das Schloß* into an allegory of literature or, more exactly, for his own view of literature. In a certain sense his reflections on *Das Schloß* recall Politzer's on "Von den Gleichnissen" (On Parables) when he asserted that all Kafka ever managed to know authoritatively was that the incomprehensible is incomprehensible. Blanchot takes a more affirmative attitude to this knowledge than Politzer does. For Blanchot literature is the voice of nothingness, paradoxically making itself known to us. What he offers, then, is not a way of understanding *Das Schloß* but a philosophical explanation for the necessity of its supreme unintelligibility — *Das Schloß* as the primal novel.

Quixotic K.

Blanchot's castle essay was occasioned by his reading of a book by Marthe Robert entitled *L'Ancien et le Nouveau de Don Quichotte à Franz Kafka* (1963; *The Old and the New*, 1977), a study of *Don Quixote* and *Das Schloß*. Robert, too, seeks to avoid the many pitfalls of conventional allegory. Consequently, she anchors her reflections in more stable, less wishfully subjective ground than most critics before her had. Her strategy, anticipating Blanchot's but not nearly so radical as his, is to shift the dialogue with Kafka away from biography and the usual allegorical referents (religion, politics, psychoanalysis) in order to explore it as literature. For Robert, the novel, undefined and undefinable, is the modern genre par excellence. It has an objective history and autonomous identity transcending Kafka's life and intentions and therefore offers itself as a congenial perspective from which to engage Kafka with relative confidence.

And if the novel is for Robert the most typical modern narrative mode, two of its supreme manifestations are *Don Quixote* and *Das Schloß*. *The Old and the New* explores the rich relationship between them. Both are quest novels that depict a protagonist whose strange venture is to him self-evident, though to the reader it is baffling. Both novels rely on a straightforward language that is descriptively realistic. Both make much of a complex dialectic between humor and seriousness, between the rational and irrational, the banal and the marvelous, and real life and mere fiction. In addition, they share an ambiguously placed narrator who seems to be and not be the hero at the same time. Finally, a crucial ambiguity lies at the heart of both novels. Are K. and his ancestor, the unhinged hidalgo of La Mancha, classic representatives of a futile, irresponsible idealism? Or are they not much more the heroic embodiments of single-minded visionaries who renew the ancient chivalric spirit under the impossible circumstances of our fallen modernity?

All these features provide Robert and her reader with rich and fruitful terrain to explore. But she adds yet another compelling observation that links Cervantes to Kafka. She shrewdly establishes subtle congruence between the authors and their protagonists. It is not simply that both identify with their heroes, which in any case is plain enough, but that both heroes act according to the same principle that guides their authors: imitation. Don Quixote consciously imitates the heroes of chivalric romances, and Cervantes writes a novel that imitates romance in the mode of parody. The protagonist, as imitator, doubles the writer, reflects a certain aspect of his identity or, more exactly (since personal biography is not the issue here), his creative undertaking. Don Quixote's way of living is really a way of writing because it is modeled on writing. K. is less obviously driven by writing, but Robert sees his supposed profession, land surveying, as an allusion to writing. It makes of K. a failed artist, for the exact art of surveying, as we are told in the novel, is one he cannot practice (because he does not have the necessary tools) and is in any case not much in demand around the castle. "As a failed writer," writes Robert,

> the last quixotic hero is an imposter, a shrewd adventurer who demands a following but does not offer the slightest justification for his exorbitant pretensions. True, his madness has not changed, but unfortunately it makes him dangerous, or at the very least, suspect. (1963:18)

Don Quixote's squire (and alter ego) Sancho Panza is doubly doubled in K.'s twin assistants. Sancho plays earthy body to Don Quixote's idealistic mind. Similarly, the two helpers give allegorical form to the somatic half of the conflict between the spirit and the body in *Das Schloß*. They embody the claims of the flesh, which goes a long way toward explaining why they are ubiquitous during K.'s lovemaking with Frieda and why one of them becomes her lover after K. and eventually destroys her feeling for him. K., like the writer he doubles, rejects the flesh as an obstacle to spiritual fulfillment, an abstract goal represented in his quixotic obsession with the castle (itself an image with antecedents in *Don Quixote*).

K. himself, a faceless, nameless outsider with no past to define him, can take shape in our imagination only against the background of literary history and the models it supplies. We have K. the manipulative womanizer from the novel of manners (Rastignac, Julien Sorel); or K. the liberator and champion of justice for the weak, a stock figure of popular serial fiction; or K. the folk hero from some far-away place, a mysterious stranger absorbed in his mission against a castle in an enchanted land, where nothing is as it seems (folk and fairy tales); K. the seeker of the Holy Grail in the footsteps of Perceval and Parzifal, an ascetic who must undergo fearful trials and is ready to renounce all to accomplish his sacred task (Count West-West as wounded Fisher King in a land of eternal winter); or K. as crafty Odysseus, returned in disguise from years abroad to restore order to the land by driving out the loafing suitors.

It is surprising only that Robert omits the Goethean Bildungsroman from her list. The castle is easily understood as a dark parody of Goethe's Tower Society, and K. as its recalcitrant apprentice. The optimistic paradigm of *Wilhelm Meisters Lehrjahre* was a powerful shaper of aesthetic sensibility, which, as Thomas Mann's *Zauberberg* shows, was in need of ironic treatment precisely at the time Kafka was writing. *Das Schloß* "takes back" Goethe's *Lehrjahre* in much the same sense that Adrian Leverkühn (in Mann's *Doktor Faustus*) takes back Beethoven's Ninth Symphony with his cantata "Weheklag Dr. Fausti." Kafka entertained such thoughts himself. In a letter to Robert Klopstock, he wrote skeptically about the biblical Abraham, who was as ready to kill his son for God, in Kafka's view, as a waiter to bring a customer's order. But if he rode out with his son, "wouldn't he be afraid of turning into Don Quixote on the way?" wonders Kafka (June 1921). This is a powerfully suggestive clue to the satiric, parodic sensibility that underlies *Das Schloß*.

K., the empty cipher, embodies — imitates, parodies — all these models to one extent or another. Perhaps Robert is not entirely persuasive on this point. Kafka does not present K. as an imitator in the same sense that Cervantes presents Quixote as a mind obsessed with following literary models. In the long view, though, she is probably right. We know that Kafka himself was obsessed with writing: he infamously declared to his luckless fiancée at various times that his whole life was literature and that it left room for nothing else (F 444). He wanted her to know that marriage to him would be a big mistake on her part and that it was up to her to break away before she took the fatal step into certain misery. That his K., plainly an extension and amplification of Kafka's self in many ways, should also be woven from many strands of the literary tradition — as both their summa and their obliteration — does not seem at all far-fetched. "Ich bin Ende oder Anfang," he wrote plausibly of his cultural predicament, meaning that he was either the last of a tradition or the founder of a new one. From the perspective that Marthe Robert offers, the declaration would apply especially to *Das Schloß*, as a book that nourishes itself on the novel genre's sources in parody yet also forcefully signals the limit of the genre.

In the background of Robert's argument one senses the presence of Georg Lukács. In his *Theorie des Romans* (1916) Lukács had described the novel's historical trajectory as a path of cultural decline. Starting with the rise of the market economy (and the scientific worldview), the spiritual unity of European culture began to disintegrate. Lukács writes not of evolution or transformation but of degeneration. In literature this meant the unraveling of traditional myth and epic. Out of the wreckage of classical epic emerged the novel, an ironic, formally fragmented, and subjective literary form. Lukács read its rise as the expression of lost cultural innocence because the novel is no longer grounded in the shared communal belief and collective unity of the Golden Age. Hermann Broch expounded similar views in his novel *The Sleepwalkers* (1930–32). That Kafka may have subscribed to some variant of this widespread cultural pessimism is likely enough, even if he did not systematically ponder the history of the European novel and its place in the masterplot of cultural disintegration.

In his diaries and letters Kafka insisted on the negativity of his historical moment — meaning perhaps only his lifetime but perhaps also all of modernity. In any case fictional works such as *In der Strafkolonie*, *Ein Landarzt*, and *Das Schloß* lend themselves handily to the gloomiest generalizations of Central European cultural despair. Robert takes *Das Schloß* to be an expression of what she considers "by now" to have become the most impossible of quixotic longings: a work of art that captures and comprehends the totality of human existence. As evidence for her large claim she adduces the problem of language. The language of *Das Schloß* is purged of the lyric mode. This is because no shred of lyric beauty remains in the diminished world into which K. has stumbled. More important, though, according to Robert, is the autonomous status of fiction itself. The work of art in the modern era is no longer an integral, noninterchangeable piece of experience. It serves no definite function, which means that the novelist, like K., lacks a true calling. The vocation of the epic bards no longer exists. Kafka's personal relation to the German language exacerbates the writer's cultural predicament. As a German-speaking Jew living in Czech Prague, Kafka was a stranger in his own country and, in a certain sense, in his own language. His nostalgia for Yiddish (which was not a part of his family life) and Hebrew (which he studied only in his last years) are an index to his sense of alienation within the language of which he was a rare master.

Robert subscribes to the dubious view, widespread among Kafka critics, that the German of Kafka's Prague was somehow inferior to the German spoken elsewhere. It was supposedly abstract and corrupted, especially as spoken by the assimilated Jews who had arrived from Galicia one or two generations earlier. Whatever impact the Jewish immigration into the city may have had on its German, it is implausible that Prague, a city of longstanding German tradition and with close links to Vienna and Berlin, should have suffered linguistically within its thriving community of German speakers. A good test case is Grete Reiner's translation of Hašek's *Good Soldier Schweik* (Hašek 1926). Her translation of the Czech relies heavily on the demotic idiom of German-speaking Prague and gives a good idea of its vigor. Kafka's literary idiom is unique, but not because he distilled it from a defective mother tongue. Robert is no doubt closer to the mark when she asserts that the singular qualities of his style in some degree related to his profession as a lawyer and the characteristics of good legal prose: clarity, specificity, and neutrality, but also monotony.

In *Das Schloß*, as elsewhere in his fiction, Kafka's curiously affectless style flattens out character and personality, class and origin, even age and education. Little Hans expresses himself in the same clear, direct prose that Momus and Pepi and Bürgel use. Figurative language is applied sparingly. As a result, it stands out in sharp relief when it does occur, for example when Gardena likens K. to a "Blindschleiche" or blindworm — a reptile that crawls on its belly — suggesting that K. lacks the superior perspective of the eagle-like Klamm.

Kafka's style also joins bureaucratic language to epic vision, and he thereby creates a uniquely ambiguous and comic effect. Simple words begin to vibrate with unexpectedly complex meanings. The word *Herr*, for example, used to refer to the castle officials (*Beamter*), can mean "lord," "bourgeois gentleman," or "master"; or, because in the novel it is sometimes interchangeable with *Beamte*, it can also mean "bureaucrat." The effect that Kafka achieves is such that it is impossible to decide whether the divine is mocked as merely bureaucratic or whether the bureaucratic has been elevated to a terrifying, almost divine power. In the same vein we might wonder whether the castle bestows its aura on the village or whether the village bestows upon the passive castle the power it only seems to possess.

It seems to me that the logic of Robert's argument should lead to the conclusion that K., like Don Quixote, cannot tell the difference between fiction and reality. In addition, it seems that Kafka amplifies the quixotic dilemma by maneuvering his reader into sharing K.'s limited point of view. We have no Sancho Panza to call things by their true names, so K.'s madness becomes our own. But Robert's point is somewhat different. In the modern, demystified world, the realm of enchanted castles persists only in the degraded form of meaningless rules and taboos with nothing but habit behind them. The rigid adherence of villagers and officials to their impenetrable code of behavior masks the underlying caprice of the empty system. Once nothing is sa-

cred, virtually anything is liable to be. When the castle officials visit the
village, everything they touch there retains their pseudo-aura: the inn
in which they sleep and eat, the women they bed, even the brutal servants they employ. But the aura is false, so the *Herrenhof,* scene of official comings and goings, becomes a caricature of castle authority, a
place in which the low and the vulgar intermingle with the supposedly
high and mighty.

K. is unable to distinguish rank and nuance in the village. His two
assistants, indistinguishable to him, are distinct to every villager. Village dress codes baffle him. He overestimates the prestige of Barnabas
implied by his costume and underestimates the power of his drably
decked out assistants. What seems normal to the inhabitants is opaque
to him, confusing and dispiriting. His solution to his quandary moves
him into the realm of quixotic delusion. He invests Klamm with practically divine powers and takes an ordinary barmaid, Frieda, for Klamm's
noble consort. Instead of doing the sensible thing — finding some
useful job in the village — K. takes on the quixotic task of challenging
the castle to a duel. But the castle's existence as the seat of all power is
far from certain. The village, with its superstitious fear of and respect
for the castle and its officials, may itself propagate an imaginary power,
or a power that once existed but now survives only through force of
habit, the insane tradition of its bureaucracy and language. The supposed castle, after all, is not a castle as far as K. can see, and he is a
keen observer. It is instead a ramshackle clutch of low buildings. But,
with everyone else, he accepts the word "castle" and all the vague
connotations that go along with it. The sign of his quixotry is his willingness to treat ordinary places — the *Herrenhof,* for example — as sacred shrines, the most banal figures (like Klamm) as lofty potentates,
the lowliest women as their queen consorts.

The survival of archaic law as meaningless vestige is of course important elsewhere in Kafka's fiction — for example, in "Zur Frage der
Gesetze" (NS 2:270). His novella *In der Strafkolonie* describes a world
in which the sadistic regime of the long dead Old Commandant has
degenerated into empty ritual: the "crime" for which the victim has
been sentenced to death by torture is that he did not fulfill his obliga-
tion to continually jump up and salute a closed door. The hunger artist
of "Ein Hungerkünstler" is devoted to an art form that has lost its
meaning over time. The emperor and his castle in "Beim Bau der Chinesischen Mauer" (The Great Wall of China) are so distant to the
builders of the Great Wall that imperial messages can never reach
them. We may assume this leaves them, like the people in the village

below the castle, to work out for themselves as best they can the laws and taboos, rights and privileges that apply to them. The word Kafka uses in the narrative's concluding parable is *erträumen*: we must dream up "the imperial message" for ourselves: *du aber erträumst sie dir* ("Eine kaiserliche Botschaft").

Each of these works belongs to Kafka's late period (1917–1924), and recalls the situation of K. in *Das Schloß*. The news of K.'s appointment to the post of surveyor evidently occurred many years before he was summoned, if he was summoned at all. The old document in question, which the village superintendent and his wife Mizzi try to find in chapter five, is lost. In a passage far too long and complex to cite, the superintendent explains to K. the temporal and bureaucratic confusions attendant upon the appointment of that surveyor whom, as he assures K., the village needed neither then nor now. The missing document, like the imperial message of "Beim Bau der Chinesischen Mauer," is one that will never arrive. K.'s appointment will remain permanently pending, a nonmessage underscored by the curiously ambivalent status of the letter Klamm sends to K. Though this document actually arrives, the message, its meaning, never does: K. cannot understand it. Authoritative order seems ubiquitous, yet that order never becomes visible. This spiritual confusion, proposes Robert, is one of the latent realities of Kafka's time. But she does not develop her point or explain why she limits it to Kafka's time and excludes, presumably, our own.

Such minor discrepancies notwithstanding, Robert's view of the novel remains richly persuasive. K.'s quest may be the quixotic pursuit of the sacred in a realm where none is to be found. The proposition brings *Das Schloß* into communication with the interwar German preoccupation with its putatively lost spirituality and the recovery of the deepest sources of European value. From the perspective of cultural despair, *Das Schloß* would be understood as a deflation of this German-European quest as quixotic. In Kafka's own life, the quixotry of his former yearning for some way to recapture his Yiddish roots must be a piece of the larger spiritual malaise he expresses in *Das Schloß*. And it amounts also to a radical questioning of the redemptive character of fiction itself. Doubt and ambiguity are the key features of Kafkan quixotry. There is no ground zero from which the reader can judge the difference between real and imaginary. Reading *Don Quixote*, we have no difficulty keeping chivalric fantasy separate from the quotidian Spanish landscape of inns and villages. Reading *Das Schloß*, however, we are obliged by the novel's narrative structure (as Robert omits to remark) to identify with the protagonist to such an extent that we can no longer tell what is true from what merely appears to be so. K.'s point of view is our own, mostly, though he probably knows a little more than we do. K. presumably knows for certain whether or not he is truly a land surveyor summoned by the castle and whether or not he is already married.

It is at least clear, as Robert does point out, that the villagers perceive the castle according to their own changing interests and desires. It is for them a mysterious, basically unintelligible force that is beyond them yet also binds them together. Most accept its power; only K. and Amalia challenge it. This power is known only through its representatives, especially Klamm, whose appearance changes depending on who is looking at him and when. It is worth noting once again that *klam* in Czech means delusion, apparition. Misperception is K.'s characteristic problem, as when he sees Barnabas's gleaming tunic and mistakes him for a person of importance. Such error and later clarification is the stitch that he repeats throughout the novel. K. is tirelessly attentive to minute details in his search for clues to the castle, but he can find no solid basis from which to judge. In this he resembles the "man from the country" in the doorkeeper parable of *Der Proceß*. The man ends by asking the fleas on the doorkeeper's fur collar for help. So it is with K. No detail is too small or absurdly trivial to conceal some crucial sign. In this vein, K. is ever alert to what people wear, thinking that outward appearance, rightly interpreted, may further his interests: Barnabas's seemingly official livery, the fine raiment of "the girl from the castle" in chapter one, the tight pants of his two helpers, and so forth. No pattern ever emerges from the sartorial chaos of castle and village, only a profusion of unconnected signs: Klamm's black frock coat and pince-nez, Frieda's boots, the landlady's vast collection of dresses.

Robert's preoccupation with signs appealed not only to Blanchot but also to Roland Barthes. In his commentary to her earlier book, *Kafka* (1960), he declares it to prove that the age of socially and politically committed literature was now past. He identifies committed art with Jean-Paul Sartre's aesthetics, whereas Robert showed that an understanding of literary technique was paramount. Kafka's truth, according to Barthes, is that "nothing but" technique is the essence of literature (Barthes 1966:140). In a chapter closely related to her study of Kafka and Cervantes, Robert begins to study imitation, which Barthes takes in support of his structuralist semiotics: only the sign, never the signified emerges. Kafka's writing, then, does not symbolize the world but alludes to the literature that has gone before, and, therefore, to literature itself.

Barthes's little essay marks an important turn in Kafka criticism, not because it was itself so influential but because it voiced early on a theme that would gradually gain force throughout the sixties and seventies in academic Kafka criticism. His semiotic reading, actually a strong misreading of Robert's purport, showed the way for later criticism that laid emphasis on the relationship between language and knowledge in Kafka's fiction. And it showed a way of bracketing out any direct concern with politics and social issues.

Nowhere in *Kafka* or in *The Old and the New* does Robert propose that Kafka's writing defines the relationship between words and world as severed. In her view, both Cervantes and Kafka offer insight into the cultural predicament of modernity. She discusses the status of women in *Das Schloß*, the concept of love, the role of art (which she sees embodied in the graceful Barnabas because he tries to carry messages between castle and village). These aspects of her books went unremarked by both Barthes and Blanchot. Even though they had less to say about *Das Schloß* than she, their general approach was more characteristic for later criticism than hers. Robert's interest in the social and historical dimension of *Das Schloß* was substantial. She develops it more fully, though with only passing remarks about *Das Schloß*, in later work (1979), in which she concentrates especially on psychoanalytically mediated reflections of Jewish themes in Kafka.

During the sixties and well into the seventies, formalist explorations of Kafka and *Das Schloß* dominated the foreground. Since in West Germany the cultural leftists seldom strayed from the Marxist-Leninist orthodoxy of the Soviet art policy, little was done to advance the positions that Adorno, above all, but also Robert had staked out. American and British Germanists remained oriented on West German criticism. The aim of Western academic criticism was to rein in the often speculative allegoresis of Kafka studies by putting it on sober, theoretically sound footing, rather than an approach dominated by psychobiographical assumptions. This meant not only ever more precise refinements in the understanding of Kafka's narrative rhetoric (for example, Sheppard 1973), but also the gradual assimilation of the French structuralist and then poststructuralist turn to language, intertextuality, and aesthetic autonomy.

Poststructural K.

In German Kafka criticism, one of the first responses to the French critical imagination came from Gerhard Kurz. Writing on Kafka and Cervantes (Robert's book had appeared in Germany in 1968) he emphasizes the self-reflexive "narrativity" and "literariness" of *Don Quixote* and *Das Schloß* together with the idea that we are, like the novels' protagonists, at all moments suspended not in an unmediated encounter with the world but in the *stories* told about the world. K.'s inability to penetrate mere appearances in order to comprehend essence is the novel's basic theme (Kurz 1975). It is a preoccupation of long standing in idealism, but projected here onto the screen of narrative. The concept *text* replaces the older, more conventional *Schein*, or appearance. At issue now is no longer allegorically cloaked ideas about history or religion, the state, or the individual, but rather narrative epistemology: the troubled link between art and reality, the word and the world.

In the United States Stanley Corngold was the first to introduce this line of thought into Kafka studies (1970). And it was a comparatist, Charles Bernheimer, who first explored *Das Schloß* from this perspective (1977). Bernheimer also emphasized the rift between text and world, one that he argues must be bridged by a "symbolic bond." More importantly, he links K.'s task to the reader's. Both must read the signs and symbols that Kafka introduces as a theme of the novel. Olga describes to K. Barnabas's account of the way messages are relayed from the castle to the village. Officials in an anteroom stand reading large books lying open on a large desk that stretches from wall to wall. The officials shift from book to book, sometimes whispering to scribes who are sitting at low benches. They constantly must jump up to hear the message, then sit down to write it up. These writings accumulate under the tables and may even be delivered if a scribe happens to recall a message addressed to someone.

Invoking Derrida, Bernheimer argues that Kafka's text describes the castle's "textuality" as a "displacement, fragmentation, postponement, duplicity" that originates in those books on the table, which in turn "are indicative of the fissure that has always-already occurred in some hypothesized original, unified text, the indelible inscription of a paternal Logos." As other instances of Derridian semiosis that permanently defers meaning, Bernheimer offers the scene in which files are distributed at the Herrenhof, the humming and singing on the telephone ("undifferentiated murmur of language engaged in its own temporal process"), Klamm's protean appearance ("capacity for displacement and substitution"), and the interchangability of Artur and Jeremias.

Bernheimer's essay does not, in fact, deconstruct Kafka's text. Instead it offers *Das Schloß* as a deconstructive text, which it surely is, since it dismantles the traditional (Romantic) assumption that the literary work of art can make present the transcendent object of desire (beauty, truth, meaning, the absolute) that is otherwise unavailable. *Das Schloß* — meaning for both K. and the reader — will remain permanently out of reach.

Two years after Bernheimer's essay, Henry Sussman published a book of deconstructive essays on Kafka, including one that fastens itself to *Das Schloß* (1979). Sussman's theme is the idea that writing inquires into and deconstructs its own processes of signification, though he attributes the "inquiry" not to language itself but to Kafka's conscious design. Nevertheless, Sussman claims that his aim is to liquidate "a certain subjectivity" — whether on the part of Kafka, his fictional protagonist, or the commentator — that contaminates the reading of Kafka's work with the residues of human activity (that is, historical, biographical, and other extralinguistic experience). The subjective contingencies of viewpoint are to be dispersed into the rhetorical mechanics of literary language.

In large part, Sussman means by subjectivity the same thing Politzer did when he described Kafka criticism as a Rorschach exercise in self-allegory. Unlike Politzer, the poststructuralist Sussman believes subjectivity can be eliminated, a trick very much like outrunning one's shadow on a sunny day. He intends to expunge it by seeking out Derridian themes in Kafka's texts: *différance*, the impossibility of establishing origins, the "always already" of articulation and reflection, the absence of presence. In fact, *Das Schloß* lends itself well to such themes. On the futile search for origin, Sussman calls attention to K.'s eagerness, and that of the village superintendents, to find the original castle document, years lost, indicating the call for a land surveyor. The castle itself is simultaneously present and absent, and (more obscurely) Sussman attempts to link the disrupted continuum of space and time achieved, he thinks, by rhetorical means (analogy, metonymy, synecdoche, metalepsis) with the Derridean project.

However, Sussman does not escape the allegory trap. He takes Derrida's themes as his referent and ransacks the novel for pegs on which to hang it. Bernheimer, even though his essay is less coherent than Sussman's in its poststructural doctrine, is much closer to a persuasive commentary when he links K.'s quest to the reader's task.

Sussman's arguments differ from those of classic literary deconstruction, such as the ones offered by Paul de Man or Geoffrey Hartman in the 1970s, in that Sussman uses Kafka's imagery as illustrative material, as an outside confirmation of Derrida's thought rather than an exploration of its critical power. De Man and Hartman characteristically took deconstruction into Romanticism, the literary realm in which claims for the unity of finite and absolute were most entrenched. They deconstructed the claims of literary and critical discourse itself. Sussman, by contrast, seeks in *Das Schloß* an allegory of the deconstructive motion. Bernheimer seeks an allegory of reading.

More conventional Kafka criticism of the seventies also focused on Kafka's language, but with a different orientation. For German critics and their North American counterparts, a postwar critical discourse about literary language was already in place. Its locus classicus was Hugo von Hofmannsthal's fictive "Ein Brief" of 1902, of which Kafka was an enthusiastic early reader (Brod 1969:180). During the early fifties, Hermann Broch had called attention to the Chandos Letter, as it is called, and the Tübingen Germanist Richard Brinkmann introduced it into the mainstream of German literary criticism, where it rapidly became a critical topos (Brinkmann 1961). Hofmannsthal's fictitious Lord Chandos experiences a crisis of language that leads him to reflect on the limits of literary expression. Kafka — who also inhabited the Austrian climate of cultural crisis that produced the radical language skepticism of Ludwig Wittgenstein, Fritz Mauthner, Karl Kraus, and others — meditated on limits of language and literary expression. These meditations — mostly in his diaries and parables — lent themselves well to becoming a foundation for the exegesis of his works (Sokel 1978, 1979; Kessler 1983).

Apart from the connection implied by his place in the timeframe of Austrian cultural history and its crisis of representation, which is only a part of the larger European picture that includes the language critiques of Nietzsche and Saussure, Kafka's narrative technique itself calls attention to the idea that language is no neutral medium. Instead, it is a perspective that inevitably imposes form on its object. The world outside the individual and collective self passes through the filter of language before it becomes conscious knowledge or, indeed, in order to become conscious knowledge. This much has become a received idea since the literary epistemology of the seventies: language structures our perception of the world. Kafka's narrative technique exploits this insight in the way it limits and structures the reader's perception of the fictional wordscape.

But the problem that seems most to have vexed Kafka himself is somewhat different. In his diaries, aphorisms, and parables he liked to ponder the reach of language toward what is beyond the senses, what he vaguely referred to as "die geistige Welt." He may have meant the inner world of his personal subjectivity, as many have argued (Beißner 1972). But it seems more likely that he had much more in mind. In one of the most famous passages from his diary (August 6, 1914), Kafka talks about representing his inner life: "Der Sinn für die Darstellung meines traumhaften inneren Lebens hat alles andere ins Nebensächliche gerückt . . . ." The key word here is *Darstellung*, the "representation" of his dreamlike inner life. The problem of representing inner life involves bridging the gap between private unmediated experience and conventional, even worn-out public language (which includes the medical discourse of psychology).

> Was in der körperlichen Welt lächerlich ist in der geistigen möglich. Dort gilt kein Schwerkraftsgesetz, (die Engel fliegen nicht, sie haben nicht irgendeine Schwerkraft aufgehoben, nur wir Beobachter der irdischen Welt wissen es nicht besser zu denken) was allerdings für uns nicht vorstellbar ist, oder erst auf einer hohen Stufe. Wie kläglich ist meine Selbsterkenntnis, verglichen etwa mit meiner Kenntnis meines Zimmers . . . . Warum? Es gibt keine Beobachtung der innern Welt, so wie es eine der äußern gibt. Psychologie ist wahrscheinlich in der Gänze ein Anthropomorphismus, ein Annagen der Grenzen. (NS2, 31–32)

> [What in the body's world is ridiculous is possible in the mind's. No law of gravity is in force there (the angels don't fly, they haven't suspended some kind of gravity, it's just that we observers from the earthly world are helpless to grasp it otherwise), which, to be sure, is beyond our power of imagination, or at least unavailable until a higher stage. How pitiful my knowledge of self when compared, for example, with my knowledge of my room. Why? There is no observation of the inner world as there is of the outward one. On the whole, psychology is probably an anthropomorphism, a nibbling at the borders.]

His approach to the dilemma, adumbrated in one of the most famous passages on language in his notebooks, offer figurative language as the solution:

> Die Sprache kann für alles außerhalb der sinnlichen Welt nur andeutungsweise, aber niemals auch nur annähernd vergleichsweise gebraucht werden, da sie entsprechend der sinnlichen Welt nur vom Besitz und seinen Beziehungen handelt. (NS2, 59)

[Language can only be used to intimate things outside the sensory world. It can never be used comparatively, not even approximately, because language in its correspondence to the sensory world deals only with property and its relations.]

Language manages well enough to pin down the empirical world, Kafka says, but it does not lend itself to authoritative representation of what lies beyond the empirical. His contrast of his self-knowledge to his knowledge of his room illustrates the point. Still, it is difficult to understand clearly what Kafka means by opposing *vergleichsweise* (comparatively) to *andeutungsweise* (hinting at, intimating). The gist of it must be the idea that some very tentative gesturing at the super-sensible "beyond" is possible. Moreover, it is reasonable to suppose that he was attempting to accomplish something of the sort in works like *Das Schloß*.

If this is so, then the complex relationship between K. and castle must be understood as an intimation of "the spiritual world" — that is, the realm of the mind, whether it be something as narrow as Kafka's personal inwardness or something as encompassing and manifold as the modern spiritual situation. In either case, and in all cases in between, Kafka cannot capture his meaning in words the way an entomologist might catch a live beetle, smother it, and pin it to a labeled board. This is the path of psychology, a nibbling at the border. Literature, as Kafka wrote in 1922 at a time when he was on the cusp of beginning *Das Schloß*, is an "Ansturm gegen die Grenze" (T 878), not a nibbling but a way of taking it by storm. Kafkan allegory reaches for the depths. The kind of knowledge Kafka is after is alive and changing (which suggests a way of understanding why Klamm always looks different). To fix a permanent name to it would falsify it. This insight is one that Kafka has in common with Musil (Dowden 1986) and Wittgenstein (Cooper 1991).

5: The New Cultural Critique

SOMEWHERE AROUND THE mid-seventies, a shift in the dominant current of modernist studies began to take shape as a reaction to the formalist preoccupations of structuralism and poststructuralism. In one sense the shift signaled a return to the earlier concerns for the embeddedness of literature in history and society and a renewal of cultural critique. But the principles and methods were new (drawing heavily on postmodern mediations of Nietzsche, Marx, and Freud), as were the aims of the critics. They began to treat works of art more suspiciously, especially the canonical ones. Demoted from the romantic-sounding term *work of art* to the more professionally detached-sounding *text*, a piece of modernist writing was taken less as the scene of subversion and critique and more as a cultural artifact, oozing false consciousness where aura used to be, and in need of crisply impartial demystification.

In the new cultural critique the emphasis falls on the hidden, frequently reactionary power relations latent in what the critics of the forties and fifties had taken to be culturally *subversive* works of art. Modernism itself, and not just certain unsavory figures — such as Pound, Benn, or Céline — but the discourse of high modernism as cultural praxis, suddenly appeared to be complicit in some of the most insidiously oppressive dimensions of the twentieth-century experience: fascism, colonialism, racism, sexism, and imperialism. Modernism was unquestionably a European, male-dominated cultural phenomenon, with the interests of Western civilization at its controlling center.

Given the prevailing climate of opinion in such matters, it is somewhat surprising that Kafka has not figured more prominently as one of the canonical figures deeply implicated in the conservative discourse of modernism. Günther Anders warned of Kafka's culturally conservative implications (1970 and 1984). Yet his criticism has only been influential for his views on Kafka and metaphor, as it was picked up and developed in new directions by Stanley Corngold (1970) and others during the seventies. Anders's cultural criticism of Kafka's fiction has found, so far as I have been able to determine, no followers.

Yet Kafka's fiction, perhaps especially *Das Schloß*, shows a distinct affinity for the kind of politically culpable cultural despair that has been widely and persuasively associated with the Weimar era (for example,

Barnouw 1988). A reading of *Das Schloß* along these lines is not hard to imagine. The novel could be said to depict modern men and women — that is, us — trapped in monstrously inauthentic lives, so inauthentic, in fact, that even the erotic — which we might reasonably hope to be the last inalienable stronghold of human spontaneity, pleasure, and freedom — is administered from above. Without much effort, Amalia's inner exile can be explained as simple resignation, the lot of modern women unwilling to bend to the absolute demands of male authority. K.'s "Faustian" striving can be seen as pitifully inadequate, perhaps the definitive failure of rationality and individual agency. And the villagers, embodying the benighted masses, are presented as people in desperate need of redemption from some outside source.

Indeed, political and spiritual redemption, often commingled inextricably, are the ubiquitous themes of conservative modernism. They usually converge in a call for outside intervention. Since God, the traditional source of redemption, has withdrawn from view, the modernist imagination leaves people to shift for themselves in a state of existential disorientation and alienation. Therefore the call is directed to a Führer figure of some sort. K. is still perceived by many as a messianic figure of this kind, a man who has come to show the way to freedom.

Why has Kafka's fiction been exempted from such criticism as I have just sketched? It is tempting to suggest that his Jewish identity has shielded him from any attempt to connect him with the intellectual forces that aided, intentionally or not, the rise of fascist ideology. But counterexamples come readily to mind. Hermann Broch's Jewish identity has not preserved him from the charge that his intellectual project was complicit in the cultural mythology of Weimar conservatism (Barnouw 1988). In this connection, we might also point toward the heavy Jewish involvement in the concept of the Salzburger Festspiele, a deeply conservative turn toward the redemptive energies of traditional art. Hofmannsthal and his allies founded the festival in the hope that art could preserve Austria after the catastrophe of the First World War had destroyed its political tradition, identity, and historical continuity.

Kafka, Hofmannsthal's "other," showed no such faith in the larger redemptive potency of art, politics, or religion. Kafka's element is negation, ironic detachment, and corrosive skepticism; and precisely these qualities of temperament and intellect save him from being just another writer of the conservative revolution, driven by metaphysical need to embrace false gods. Food and health fads (he was a vegetarian follower of Horace B. Fletcher's pseudoscientific regime of chewing and digestion) seem to mark the outer limit of Kafka's radicalism. Wary critical detachment is Kafka's more usual mode of thought.

Uncompromising skepticism distinguishes Kafka and *Das Schloß* from the common run of the Weimar Era's redemptive obsessions. The spiritual vacuum of Central European spiritual and intellectual life after the First World War was fertile ground for theories of aesthetic redemption, charismatic leaders, and religious boondoggles of every sort. New mythologies sprang up like toadstools after a long rain. Kafka, who like his hunger artist never found the "food" that he liked, resisted them and the phony redemption they promised.

Moreover, he sought no redemption in art either. He viewed the artist as a hedonist absorbed in the pleasures of writing, alienated from life for purely selfish reasons (MBFK 2:376–80). He gives the same thoughts a fictional form in his final tale, "Josefine die Sängerin, oder Das Volk der Mäuse" (1924). Josefine, the vain artist, is no leader for the "masses" of mouse folk, and her art belongs to the moment, not to eternity. She claims to be a savior of the people, but the story's narrator dismisses her claim as piffle. If she offers redemption, it is a very brief one, which takes place only while the mouse folk are listening to her song.

> Freilich sie rettet uns nicht und gibt uns nicht die entscheidenden Kräfte, es ist leicht sich als Retter dieses Volkes aufzuspielen . . . das sich noch immer irgendwie selbst gerettet hat . . . . Und doch ist es wahr, daß wir gerade in Notlagen noch besser als sonst auf ihre Stimme horchen. (NS2:662)

> [Of course she does not redeem us and does not bestow upon us the crucial powers. It is easy to play the savior of this people . . . that has always managed somehow to redeem itself . . . . And yet it is also true that precisely in dangerous situations we listen more closely to her voice than any other time.]

The concepts *Führer* and *Retter* are cognate here. Josefine is admired, but not as a savior. She offers consolation, not redemption. The mouse-folk's interaction with her gives a wholesomely restrained view of art and its place in modern culture. The tenor of the Weimar era's attitude was much different. The title of Max Kommerell's 1928 classic of cultural conservatism, *Der Dichter als Führer*, is a better indicator of the spirit of the times than anything Kafka wrote. Outsize writer-celebrities dominated in the Weimar and European firmament of stars. Kafka's tough-minded reserve is uncharacteristic of the aesthetic era that produced Joyce and Proust, Eliot and Pound, Brecht and Jünger, Thomas Mann and Robert Musil.

All of these writers entertained grandiose ideas about the exalted place of art in culture: its political, or religious, or near-religious meaning and potential for regenerating the lost Golden Age or bringing about the coming era. Heidegger's messianic view of Hölderlin is probably the most instructive example of the Weimar era's hypertrophied vision of art and the artist. By contrast, Kafka views the writer as alienated and narcissistic. The Kafkan artist is figured as the forgotten hunger artist, as the acrobat who refuses to come down from his trapeze, as a squeaking mouse-singer, and as a burrowing beastie that lives in utter solitude in a world of his own making. These images give us a gently ironic version of the modern artist and his or her virtually nonexistent potential for radical influence. Kafka's artist is emphatically not Max Kommerell's aesthetic Führer, and his art is not the redemptive stuff of Hofmannsthal's Festspiele.

Kafka's modest claims about art places the contemporary Kafka critic in an interestingly two-sided position. Though Kafka renounced the idea of the artist as a leader-redeemer in dark times, he has ironically become one of the most authoritative figures of modernism. It is in part the tension between Kafka's aesthetic modesty (usually glossed by postwar interpreters as the sign of his existential authenticity) and his colossal prestige that undercuts the attempt to read him as just another apostle of Central European cultural despair. If his K., to name the salient case, sometimes seems like a messianic figure, it should serve only to throw the category of messiah and Führer into doubt.

There are other consequences for the collision between Kafka's modest claims for art and his outsize reputation. It makes his place in the divagating rhizome-like structure of cultural critique as practiced since the late seventies significantly and characteristically protean. Kafka's prestige as one of the canonical titans of high modernism makes his fiction automatically suspect. Yet as a marginal, barely known writer living in a provincial capital, himself a member of an oppressed minority, he can — or his advocates can — stake his claim to have been a keen critic of the oppressive structures that cultural critique aims to lay bare. Let us turn first to the view from feminism, which is the most conflicted perspective on Kafka.

The View from Feminism

Criticism that seeks to interrogate modernism as a discourse does not usually concentrate its attention on individual texts. One aim of feminist literary criticism is to recover alternative modernisms and juxtapose them to the dominant, mostly male, pantheon. Writers of the Anglo-American tradition such as Gertrude Stein and H.D. no longer figure as mere footnotes to the Pound era. They have come into their own as writers representative of an alternative canon. The Harlem Renaissance, too, belongs within the now larger and changing perception of literary modernism. In German studies a feminist reappraisal of the tradition has been under way for some time now, but it has concentrated its attention principally on women of the Romantic era. Feminine and feminist modernism has not fared so well. Within the parameters of modernist writing, no women writers have yet been submitted to the thoroughgoing reevaluation and new prestige enjoyed, for example, by Bettina von Arnim, Sophie von La Roche, and Rahel Varnhagen in Romanticism or Gertrude Stein and Zora Neale Hurston in American modernism. Even Else Lasker-Schüler remains a curiously marginal presence.

Kafka has received his due share of attention. When the practitioners of German studies view Kafka from the perspective of feminism, both *Das Schloß* and *Der Proceß* come into view, mainly because of the protagonists' disturbed relationships with women. K. and Josef K. both show a marked tendency to be drawn into erotic relationships at awkward moments. Women, simultaneously submissive and aggressive, are their seducers and, consequently, their downfall. For example, when Josef K. visits the lawyer Huld and should be focusing all his powers of concentration on his case, he allows himself to be drawn aside by the spontaneously affectionate Leni, Huld's web-fingered maid. In a neighboring room they fall into passionate embraces on the floor beneath the portrait of one of the court's judges. Significantly, the judge appears outraged and on the verge of handing down a verdict.

Love, as Freud once pointed out, is wet. And as Walter Benjamin and Adorno both pointed out, Leni's webbed fingers suggest that she is the distant descendant of some primal swampland creature (Benjamin 1981:28-9). Her impulsive sexuality — warm, wet and slimy (by extension of the "swamp" metaphor) — makes her a little less than human or, at best, less than a moral-rational agent. If we draw out Kafka's metaphor into an explanatory form, it warns that the pleasures of female sexuality are perilous to rational man, a bog that threatens to trap and devour the unlucky male who, straying from the path of reason, wanders into it.

The situation in *Das Schloß* is similar but not identical. Like Leni before her, Frieda is presented as a temptress. This time, however, the danger of female sexual domination is more directly figured. Frieda is a whip-wielding dominatrix. When K. first meets her, he witnesses the tavern scene in which she takes up a whip to halt Klamm's servants as they dance lewdly around Olga, the village whore. Though Frieda herself almost succumbs to the sexual pull of the dance, or so it seems to K., she finally masters her will and drives Klamm's insatiable menservants back into the sty "where they belong," as she puts it (S 65). Mythic or at least mythological echoes are audible. Sexual hunger turns men into feral, grunting pigs: Klamm's Dionysian servants gurgle hungrily ("hungrig röchelnd") as they paw Olga. The Homeric enchantress, Circe, turned men into pigs; Frieda, her distant descendant, has complete control over them as she drives them into their pen. Such scenes link Kafka, we should note in passing, to the primitivist expressionists. One can easily imagine a painting of this scene rendered in the style of Emil Nolde's *Dance around the Golden Calf* (1910) or his *Mary of Egypt* (1912).

At first glance K. is in control of the scene. He propositions Frieda, asking to spend the night with her, and she submits to his will, or seems to. Attentive reading reveals another story. As so often happens in Kafka's fiction, word and image contest each other, with image as the more powerful modality of expression. K. controls the scene verbally, but it is Frieda, the whip-girl, who has her "little" foot on a supine K.'s chest while he is hiding from the landlord under her bar. Working on a separate and deeper stratum than rational language, the imagery presents the woman with distinctly sadistic overtones and the man as masochist. Visually, the nearness of the scene to pornographic kitsch is unmistakable.

The famous lovemaking scene between K. and Frieda, which is also fraught with colliding themes, remains within the framework of the struggle for dominance and control. Frieda lies on the floor, her beckoning arms open in a seemingly passive invitation, but when K. fails to respond to her blandishments, she seizes control:

> Dann schrak sie auf, da K. still in Gedanken blieb, und fing an wie ein Kind an ihm zu zerren: "Komm, hier unten erstickt man ja," sie umfaßten einander, der kleine Körper brannte in K.'s Händen, sie rollten

in einer Besinnungslosigkeit, aus der sich K. fortwährend aber verge-
blich zu retten suchte, ein paar Schritte weit, schlugen dumpf an
Klamms Tür und lagen dann in den kleinen Pfützen Bieres und dem
sonstigen Unrat, von dem der Boden bedeckt war. (S 68)

[Then she came up with a start, since K. remained in silent thought,
and began grabbing at him like a child: "Come on, we could smother
down here." They clamped themselves together; her little body burned
in K.'s hands. With a reckless abandon, from which K. continually but
unsuccessfully tried to rescue himself, they rolled a few steps to the
side, banging against Klamm's door with a thud, and then lying in the
little puddles of beer and other filth that covered the floor.]

That climactic thump against Klamm's door is Kafka's gross image of a
guilty orgasm. It is reminiscent of the jismatic stream of cars that gush
across the bridge at the end of "Das Urteil" (The Judgment). In Kafka's fiction, sexual pleasure is always an outrage, a filthy distraction
from serious business, proof of the protagonist's weakness and moral
failure. Nevertheless, women take the blame for it, for they are above
all soulless, sensual creatures who prey on the male's susceptibilities.

Like Leni, Frieda commands the protagonist sexually. She casts her
spell on a K. who is unable to resist her, even though he struggles
against the grip of the sexual pleasure she represents. He "continually"
tries to free himself from the condition to which she has reduced him.
Her swampy element is the effluvia of the tavern floor. They spend
hours there together, and during that whole time K. feels like a lost
but happy soul. However, when Klamm calls out for Frieda, and when
she defiantly resists his summons ("Ich bin beim Landvermesser! Ich
bin beim Landvermesser!"), K. instantly regrets his lack of self-control.
Frieda, who, like Leni, may be an agent of the authorities whom K.
hopes to master, has deflected him from his mission. She has perhaps
even spoiled his chances for success. If she really is Klamm's concu-
bine, then K. may have permanently damaged his own interests. Now
that the damage is done, though, K. looks to his own advantage. Like
the ever-resourceful Odysseus, K. attempts to profit from the unexpected turn of events. The machinations of his devious mind are in-
sinuated in the text, but they are explicit in a deleted passage. His new
lover is not first in his postcoital reveries:

K. dachte mehr an Klamm als an sie. Die Eroberung Friedas ver-
langte eine Änderung seiner Pläne, hier bekam er ein Machtmittel,
dass vielleicht die ganze Arbeiterzeit im Dorfe unnötig machte." (Sa
185)

[K. was thinking more about Klamm than about her. The conquest of Frieda called for a change of plan. Now he had found a vehicle of power that might make his stretch of time as a working man in the village unnecessary.]

Like Josef K. before him, K. seeks help from the women he also exploits: from Frieda, his mistress, who links him to Klamm; from Gardena, who houses him and advises him from her bed; from Pepi, who wants him to move in with her, and Olga and Amalia and the girl from the castle. Moreover, women may well be the true power behind the men: Gisa (Schwarzer's harsh mistress), Gardena at the Bridge Inn, the auratic girl from the castle at Lasemann's, Mizzi at the village superintendent's office. The source of their power is their sexuality. Even after they are no longer sexually appealing (Gardena and Mizzi, for example), their power has become a fact that the men do not contest. Gardena's passive husband shuffles aimlessly about the inn. He could be the image of K.'s fate if he marries Frieda.

The construction of female sexuality as a threat to male rationality, self-possession, and control places *Das Schloß* within a larger discourse of modernism that Sylvia Bovenschen has called the "imaginary femininity" (1979). Reiner Stach has similarly explored turn-of-the-century prejudices against women as they are expressed in Kafka's fiction (Stach 1987). However, there is an exception to the rule. The woman in *Das Schloß* who eludes the construction of woman as sexual man-devourer is Amalia. She is unique in Kafka's fiction, and she also offers a site at which a positive feminist Kafka criticism can unfold, one that goes beyond the ritual gesture of debunking Kafka's alleged propagation of an undesirable sexual stereotype. Marjanne E. Goozé's essay of 1983 is an interesting case in point. She takes the characteristic preoccupations of seventies-era Kafka criticism — the themes of text, textuality, and silence — and reads them through a feminist optic.

Das Schloß is awash with legible texts: protocols, signs, gestures, bundles of documents, scraps of paper, and written messages of various sorts — Klamm's letter to K., the lost summons for a surveyor, and Sortini's vile letter to Amalia, and the bit of paper left over after the ritual distribution of documents at the Herrenhof. Most of the novel's characters, especially K. but not only K., invest an effort of virtually talmudic intensity in trying to interpret castle messages correctly. The task is futile. Even if the message can be found, the chances of excavating its meaning are so remote as to be negligible. This is clear from

K.'s meeting with the village superintendent and from Barnabas's description of how castle scribes pass on messages.

The only figure who grasps the futility is Amalia. She recognizes the message-interpretation hornswoggle as a bottomless pit and refuses to play the castle's game. When Sortini's message comes to her via his courier, Amalia tears it to pieces and flings it into the messenger's face. She simultaneously rejects Sortini's sexual demand and the castle's method of asserting its authority, through "texts" or, more exactly, the endless interpretations they set into motion. The contrast between Amalia and K. is strong. He accepts sexual possession without hesitation as the basic unit of power. And where he pores over every detail of a castle "text," written or otherwise, in a vain attempt to extract a useful meaning from it, Amalia rejects the activity of interpretation altogether.

The refusal has two meanings. First, it shows that Amalia refuses to submit herself sexually to the debauched expectations of castle officialdom. She is the only woman in the village who is not a part of the master-slave ritual that goes on between men and women in the novel. She defies the status quo, asserting a moral autonomy that is unique in the novel (Dowden 1990). Second, her refusal suggests something about how the interpreting reader ought to deal with Kafka's "text," though Goozé is muddled on this point. K.'s habits of interpretation lead nowhere, obviously enough, and so should not serve the reader as a model. But, contrary to Goozé's reading, Amalia's antihermeneutic revolt, however admirable it may be, does not lead anywhere either in helping the reader understand how best to deal with Kafka's writing. If anything, her example serves as an invitation to tear up the text and withdraw into silence.

What is actually being torn to pieces in Goozé's essay is something else, something only slightly displaced. Her essay sits on the faultline between the shift from the self-referential practices of literary analysis in the post-structuralist seventies, which characteristically bracketed historical and ethical questions, toward cultural criticism, in her case the feminist boom in literary criticism of the eighties. Goozé's enthusiasm for Amalia's defiance of the castle's textuality suggests nothing so much as her own generation's rejection of a textual regime in the American academy. Goozé was a graduate student in the early eighties when she wrote her essay. It was a time when graduates were under strong peer pressure to follow the trends of the seventies, especially those stemming from the work of Derrida and de Man. The structural-poststructural paradigm and its agendas of literary analysis, by then institutionalized, insisted that there was nothing outside "the text." The principal message of Goozé's argument is that women are outside the text and will not submit to erasure.

What separates Goozé's treatment of Kafka from the more common exercises in debunking the modernist construction of women (Beck 1987; Boa 1990), is her willingness to accept *Das Schloß* as the scene of critique and not just the passive object of enlightened analysis. Amalia is a curiously unique figure in Kafka's fiction. His presentation of women in general in *Das Schloß* suggests that his fiction may after all belong to the oppressive "discourse" of modernism that is widely perceived as reactionary in its sexual politics and often, if not always, in its political unconscious. The basic problem with such views of Kafka is that they fail to account for the unique and idiosyncratic qualities of his imagination.

The Politics of Kafka and Modernism

In the late forties and early fifties, as we saw in chapter one, Günther Anders warned that Kafka's hermetic modernism was reactionary in its political implications. His minority status notwithstanding, Kafka arguably belongs to the conservative tradition of European letters. Much of the German tradition's romantic inwardness, cultural pessimism, and self-absorbed melancholy speaks from his fiction. Indeed, Kafka consciously aligned himself aesthetically with cultural conservatives, identifying with Kleist, Flaubert, Goethe, and even the early Thomas Mann. Although he outgrew the dandyism of his earliest period, Kafka did not link his writing to political life as the Mann brothers did. The First World War, Czech independence, the burning issue of democracy in Weimar and Austria scarcely made it into his notebooks and letters. And Zionism, insofar as it appears in his fiction at all, does so in a highly mediated, cryptic form.

Anders also suggested that the rage for Kafka in postwar Germany arose as a strategy of atonement that actually amounted to a way of forgetting the Holocaust (1984). Similarly, it is possible to argue that Kafka's international reputation after the war was boosted significantly by the simple fact that he was Jewish. Since he would have been a target of Nazi murderers, as indeed his works were consigned to flames by the Nazi book burners, it may be that his works have been spared the ideological criticism that some commentators lavished on other modernists. Kafka may be, in part, an "imaginary Jew" in a specific sense given to that expression by a French essayist, Alain Finkielkraut.

In an autobiographical book of 1980 Finkielkraut declared himself to be an "imaginary Jew," by which he meant he became identified by himself and others with a suffering he never experienced. As the post-1945 child of Polish Jews who survived the Holocaust, he wrote, he was the beneficiary of a special, morally superior status that he had not earned. He describes the various ways in which he exploited this specialness in order to denounce his posturing as a fantasy that depreciated the memory of those who actually suffered and perished in the Holocaust. Auschwitz has no heirs, as he pointedly observes, and we owe it to the memory of the real victims not to appropriate their suffering on behalf of mimicking the Holocaust personally or making a theater of it.

If Auschwitz has no heirs, then it has no mystic prophets either. Yet it remains difficult to separate from it Kafka's strange and extraordinary vision. "He did not live to see the Holocaust," wrote Alfred Kazin, recalling a photograph of Kafka that hung in Hannah Arendt's apartment, "though he guessed it and its aftermath" (1978:199). Kazin's reasons for claiming this are honorable, but it may be that this kind of thinking helps to obscure the right understanding of both Kafka and the Holocaust.

Even though Anders's view of Kafka in many ways anticipated the kind of ideological suspicion now associated with Fredric Jameson's concept of literature's political unconscious, only the feminists have treated Kafka's ideological subtext skeptically. Theirs is not the only game in town, of course. Contemporary cultural criticism is an undertaking wide and varied enough to accommodate a bewildering diversity of competing points of view. On the whole, cultural critique is understood to mean an analytical exploration of the ways in which imaginative writing is positioned with regard to history, politics, and religion. Let us turn first to religion, which in Kafka's case overlaps with politics.

In explorations of Kafka's political meaning, Kafka's own political unconscious has most often been sought in his complex negotiations with Judaism and his Jewish identity. The basic conflict is well known. He was raised in an assimilated middle-class household speaking standard German (with no Yiddish or Hebrew) as a nonobservant Jew in a city full of Czech and German Catholics. As a result, he felt cut off from the traditional sources of Jewish identity: language, religion, custom. Conversion to Catholicism would have been a gross self-deception, as Kafka plainly understood, for he never entertained the idea, though it was a not uncommon step among his friends and contemporaries.

Nevertheless, he also found himself unable to take the step into a commitment to religious Judaism or political Zionism. His habits of mind were too skeptical for political commitment, too secular for normative Judaism, too intellectual for fundamentalist varieties. Still, he longed for escape from anti-Semitism and for unity with his fellow Jews. From 1912 on he periodically toyed with the idea of emigrating to Palestine. But he was too self-consciously European, and in the end also too ill, to reinvent himself as pioneer. The situation left Kafka stranded between identities and, as many commentators have noted, probably conditioned the imaginary crossbreeds in some of his animal fables: the cat-lamb of "A Cross" and Odradek in "The Cares of a Family Man," and perhaps echoes in the dilemma of Rotpeter, the unhappily assimilated ape in "A Report to an Academy."

Within the narrower tradition of Kafka criticism, the concern with Kafka's Jewish identity and its meaning for his fiction has been a topic of growing scholarly interest, especially since Evelyn Torton Beck's study of his enthusiasm for Yiddish theater (Beck 1971). In the eighties, though, the topic emerged from the subdiscipline of Kafka biography to become a dominant feature of the critical landscape in Kafka scholarship. Its emergence into the mainstream reinforces what might be called Kafka's renewed claim to a subversive position, this time within the modernist canon.

One of the most radical critics to frame an image of Kafka from the religious point of view is Harold Bloom. Bloom's forceful advocacy of Kafka's fiction as a subversive interpretation of modern Judaism reverses the usual direction of critique. Most critics cautiously try to prove that Kafka knew a great deal about the various Jewish traditions: Bible, Talmud, Hasidism, Kabbalah, ritual, and so forth. Then, having shown that Kafka had a discernable interest in and specific knowledge of this or that piece of Judaism, they try to show that it somehow fed into his work. Bloom does not care much about Kafka's specific knowledge of Judaism. What interests him is Kafka's impact on the modern Jewish mind. He argues that it has been substantial enough in some ways to alter the received notions of what it means to be a Jew. It is a claim that is hard if not impossible to substantiate, yet it seems likely that Bloom is right.

Gnosticism, which Bloom attributes to Kafka's work in general and to *Das Schloß* in particular, is not a time-bound phenomenon, though

Bloom is willing to admit that it seems to him appropriate for our day. For Bloom, Kafka's style of thought bears the marks of a heretical Jewish mysticism, regardless of whether or not Kafka thought of himself as part of an identifiable ·countertradition or had any detailed knowledge of it. Kafka's fiction has turned out to be powerful enough to mount an assault on the normative tradition, change its direction for now and the future, and consequently reshape the overall cultural image of the contemporary Jew.

The contemporary secular intellectual, says Bloom, seeking the decisive image of Jewishness these days is more likely to come up with Freud and Kafka and even Gerschom Scholem than with Maimonides or Raschi or Moses Mendelssohn. Even where Kafka's influence may not be direct, Bloom suspects that his presence will be felt via influential mediators. In evidence of his proposition he adduces the decisive influence of Kafka on Walter Benjamin's and Gerschom Scholem's conceptions of Judaism. Bloom stresses the importance of Scholem in particular because he is this century's preeminent exegete and exponent of Jewish mysticism (Bloom 1988a and b).

Since Bloom cannot prove his claim (and does not think it needs any more proof than might be required to back up the comparable propositions that Milton and Dante have exercised spiritual authority), he lets it stand as his premise that Kafka has helped to stake out, as indeed a land surveyor might (if he had the right tools and know-how), the spiritual space of the Jewish people. The form of Kafka's Judaism, though, and the key to his achievement, is a spirit of negation that Bloom believes to be in the tradition of the ancient Gnostics. He regards *Das Schloß* and the rest of Kafka's related imagery (the Law, the Great Wall of China, and so forth) as embodiments of a gnostic negation that amount to an assault on normative Judaism. But he does not make the castle into an allegory for average Jewish reality. The crucial negation is not K.'s rebellion against the castle but Kafka's evasion of interpretation. The secret doctrine of Kafka's mysticism is its refusal to yield to exegesis.

The rhetorical power of Bloom's 'strong reading' of Kafka is identical with its major weakness. His view cannot be submitted to tests that would either prove or disprove it. Bloom's position is appealing perhaps most of all because it takes an imaginative literary achievement seriously as a social and even spiritual achievement, claiming for it a real and significant impact on culture. His Kafka is much more than the passive reflection of ideology. It is this side of Bloom's work that links his idiosyncratic, more or less rhetorical criticism to the realm of cultural critique, even if the convergence of interests here may be accidental.

Bloom's imagination and skill as a writer set him apart from the garden variety academic critic. Indeed, the element of fiat in his version of Kafka has kept him out of the mainstream of Kafka criticism. If conventional scholarship does not bear out his findings, Bloom is not worried. So much the worse for conventional scholarship. Instead of appealing to traditional standards of evidence, Bloom appeals to the imagination of his readers. In so doing, only he follows the example of both Benjamin and Scholem, whose Kafkas probably have been as influential as he claims. When a critic as reserved, judiciously sober, and popular as Robert Alter writes a book entitled *Necessary Angels: Kafka, Benjamin, Scholem* (1990), it can only mean that these figures have reached the general importance and acceptance that are tellingly referred to as canonical.

Conventional scholarship in the eighties is inclined in much the same direction as Bloom, laying emphasis on Kafka's Judaism, though it comes at the problem from the opposite direction. Rather than asking what Kafka means in the present, it asks what Kafka meant in his own setting, which is almost the same thing. From the hermeneutic perspective, the critic's contemporary setting is the context that really counts because it decides which issues of the past are the ones worth thinking about. Kafka's texts can respond only to the questions put to them, and the origin of the questions is almost always in the present. Cold War liberals, for example, asked questions about subversion and containment. In our era, questions of multiculturalism and authenticity pervade the public and scholarly imagination. In Europe as in North American questions of cultural identity have become increasingly pressing. It is this concern with ethnic roots versus cosmopolitan urbanity, individual versus group identity, and religious versus secular identity that underlies the turn to figures like Kafka who wrestled explicitly with the issues that are now on the intellectual agenda.

The path opposite to Bloom's, then, arrives at the same destination. Where Bloom proceeds according to the lights of his own imaginative interests, setting aside questions of provenance and intention, conventional criticism remains anchored in historical-critical research. Of the many contributions in this area during the eighties, the one that stands out is *Kafka: Judaism, Politics, Literature* (1985) by Ritchie Robertson, a British critic. Robertson deploys the armory of techniques and tools at the disposal of historical-critical literary research in order to demonstrate the substantial impact of Yiddish and, especially, Hasidic tradition on Kafka. What his efforts reveal, though, is somewhat differ-ent. Surprisingly, and contrary to Robertson's intentions, the very probity of his work proves that it remains difficult and highly conjec-tural to make compelling connections between Kafka's knowledge of Judaism and his fictional texts. It is significant that Robertson finds so little of substance. A certain amount is well known, especially with re-gard to *Das Schloß*, which was written at a time when Kafka was cer-tainly reflecting on the meaning and depth of his own Judaism. When Kafka discovered the Yiddish theater in 1911, he began to concern himself with issues of Jewish identity. He read Heinrich Graetz's *Geschichte der Juden* (History of the Jews, 1887–89), Meyer Isser Pinès's *Histoire de la littérature Judéo-Allemande* (History of Yiddish Literature, 1900), and Jakob Fromer's *Organismus des Judentums* (Organism of Jewry, 1909). He began to read Jewish journals includ-ing the Zionist weekly *Selbstwehr* and Buber's *Der Jude*.

That things Jewish helped to shape Kafka's literary imagination is beyond question. But when Robertson tries to show exactly which forces shaped which specific works, he runs into difficulty. On slim evi-dence he maintains that Hasidic tales are the source of certain themes. Georg Langer, a friend of Kafka's who had taken the plunge from Westernized urban Judaism into Galician Hasidism, was Kafka's guide. He told Kafka a few traditional tales of the Ba'al Shem Tov ("Master of the Good Name"). The Ba'al Shem, who was born Israel ben Eliezer and lived in the second half of the eighteenth century, was the founder of Hasidism. Kafka recorded Langer's anecdotes on two pages of his diary in October 1915. He also took an interest in helping Hasidic refugees from the war zone in Galicia, and his last love, Dora Dymant, was the rebellious child of Hasidic parents. It is fair to say that Kafka took a lively if detached interest in Hasidism, but little else can be claimed with confidence.

Robertson's strongest emphasis in his study of *Das Schloß* falls on the theme of messianism. That it may be a Hasidic borrowing is not a new idea. W. G. Sebald has also speculated that K. could be a figure from Hasidic folklore: the messiah as unknown wanderer who would disappear if he were recognized (1976 and 1985). However, the view does not fit the text well unless K. does not know he is the messiah. Kafka's reader is privy to most of K.'s thoughts, and there is no sign that he thinks he is the messiah. A deleted passage is explicit on the point. Olga regards him as a potential messiah of sorts, but

> Er war nicht gekommen um jemandem Glück zu bringen, es stand
> ihm frei, aus eigenem Willen auch zu helfen wenn es sich traf, aber nie-
> mand sollte ihn als Glücksbringer begrüssen; wer das tat, verwirrte
> seine Wege, nahm ihn für Dinge in Anspruch, für die er, so gezwun-
> gen, niemals zur Verfügung stand. (Sa 369)

> [He did not come in order to do anybody any good. He was free to
> help when appropriate, but nobody should consider him a bringer of
> good fortune. Whoever did so confused his paths, laid claim to him for
> purposes that, when forced on him, lay beyond him.]

If K. is a messiah, he is a pretty poor specimen. His self-seeking ill
treatment of Frieda and little Hans Brunswick and his calculating interest in Hans's frail mother do little to enhance his image to the
reader as a redemptive figure.

Robertson agrees, for he claims that *Das Schloß* serves as a critique
of the messianic tradition. But except for the most familiar examples —
that is, the Hebrew pun on *mashoah* (surveyor) and *mashiah* (messiah)
and the proposition that K.'s light-hearted, empty-headed assistants are
probably derived from Yiddish theater — Robertson is able to produce
little in the way of hard evidence to connect the novel to Jewish lore.
Kafka *may* have known this or *might* have read that. Robertson is in
the end unable to show that Kafka *did* in fact have a detailed knowledge of Hasidic lore, that the images in the novel reflect his use of it,
and that they constitute a critique. His thorough discussions eventually
succeed in persuading his reader that *Das Schloß* might be indebted to
the Hasidic world in some roundabout way but not that it *is* in any
sense a vital piece of what has connected Kafka's readers to the novel
over the years.

In his research into the background of *Das Schloß*, Robertson has
run up against the limits of the historical-critical method of scholarship
and interpretation. His aim is to establish the historically probable perspective of Kafka's intellectual horizon. His reconstruction of it is
speculative, as it must be, owing to the strangely reticent character of
Kafka's diaries and letters. As a consequence, Robertson's findings on
Das Schloß simply reconfirm familiar views of the castle: K. is probably
a phony messiah figure; the bath scene at Lasemann's may suggest ritual purification (perhaps Jewish, perhaps related to a diary entry of
October 27, 1911); Artur and Jeremias may be figurations of K.'s repressed instinct for joy; erotic love (with Frieda) may stand for a link to
the divine. Each of these may, as Robertson suggests, owe a debt to
Kafka's knowledge of Hasidism.

Still, even if the details of Kafka's knowledge and intentions cannot be reconstructed with confidence, it remains incontestable that the general issue of Judaism was central to Kafka's imaginative life. The basic issues are hidden in plain view. As Gershon Shaked notes, "his themes of emigration, the struggle to gain a residence permit, eternal wandering, persecution and guilt feelings are all typical of the Jewish condition" (1984:11). To them might be added the preoccupation with commentary, law, commandment, and tradition, all of which also figure prominently in the Jewish tradition. Hannah Arendt wrote similarly in the forties, focusing on the Jew as pariah in Kafka's fiction. Not much more can be claimed with a circumspect degree of scholarly certainty. The strategy of cultural criticism in dealing with the pervasive issue of Jewishness focuses less on historical-critical research (though cultural critics are happy to call on its findings when it happens to suit their needs) than on the ability of a given text to produce meanings in a given cultural setting (no matter whether they are supported by authorial intention or not). At issue for Robertson is Kafka's perception of himself as a writer.

Like Robertson, David Suchoff (1994) is interested in the cultural terrain bounded by Judaism, politics, and literature in Kafka's work. But Suchoff explores *Das Schloß* in a different register and with the intention of appropriating *Das Schloß* on behalf of a discourse of social change. Where Robertson assumes a traditional posture of dispassionate scholarly detachment and is concerned with establishing Kafka's probable intentions, Suchoff vigorously situates himself in contemporary discourses of ethnicity and solidarity and is concerned more with the meaning of literature as a cultural praxis than with upholding the pretense of detachment.

He sees in *Das Schloß* a classic text in which high modernism collides with popular culture. As a writer of supremely crafted narratives, writing in a standard, ethnically neutral German, Kafka is a classic high modernist in the Flaubertian tradition: universal, difficult, autonomous. But Kafka was also an unabashed enthusiast of sentimental Yiddish theater, an apologist for the Yiddish language, and an outspoken enemy of the cultural snobbery that led assimilated Western Jews to feel superior to their East European cousins. As far as Kafka was concerned, the unself-conscious confidence with which the Jews of the East led their lives gave them a superiority over the self-doubting, half assimilated, self-alienated Jews of the West. Kafka felt a distinct nostalgia for this world, the lost paradise of European Jewish identity.

Suchoff takes the idea of a Jewish identity joined to a Jewish literature as a fulcrum to leverage *Das Schloß*. "Reaching the Castle," he declares, "suggests a desire to obtain a fixed national identity" (1994:150). The impulse parallels the aims of both political and cultural Zionists in Kafka's Prague. And Kafka, even if not a committed Zionist, was in sympathy with their need to overcome the instability and indeterminacy of European Jewish identity. That he did not actively support their political goals, though, leads us to suppose that the castle is not a coded image for Zion. Theodor Herzl, Martin Buber, and Ahad Ha'am, the great contemporary theorists and activists of Jewish national identity, made little impression on Kafka. Kafka's K. registers the problem — modern anxiety, homelessness, alienation — but does not promise a solution.

In Suchoff's view, the castle represents the inherent falsity of ideology. Hence its protean, shifting, indeterminate quality. K.'s desire to enter the castle suggests to Suchoff not messianic revolt or divine grace but the self-deceiving impulse to assimilate. K. is a pariah struggling not only to gain acceptance but to become one with the powers that be. If he has left his history and identity behind, it is because he intends to become someone else. Kafka scholars never fail to note the unambiguously positive meaning of marriage in the Jewish tradition and for Kafka, whose reluctance (or failure or inability) to marry and establish a family was a source of shame. Indeed, there is nothing specifically Jewish about it; it is a universal. Bearing this in mind, we should remember that K. claims to have abandoned a wife and child (S 10). We cannot judge the truth, but either way it makes a bad impression. I believe Kafka means for his implied reader to recognize the transgression for the shabby behavior it is. That K. mentions it offhandedly, in passing, and never thinks about it otherwise only worsens the reflection on his character.

One of the oddest things about *Das Schloß* — written at a time when Kafka was strongly attracted to questions of Judaism, Jewish community, and his own Jewishness — is the utter absence of any markers of Judaism in the novel: it contains no Jews, no synagogues, no references to Yiddish, Hebrew, or anything else that might suggest its author's interests or ethnic identity. When Frieda wants to run away with K., it is not to Palestine but to Spain or southern France. When K. recalls his hometown he thinks of its church tower. The castle village has no Jewish quarter, no synagogue, no Jews recognizable as such. Yet in a diary entry of January 16, 1922, Kafka wrote this muchquoted passage:

Diese ganze Litteratur ist Ansturm gegen die Grenze und hätte sich, wenn nicht der Zionismus dazwischen gekommen wäre, leicht zu einer neuen Geheimlehre, zu einer neuen Kabbala entwickeln können. Ansätze dazu bestehn. Allerdings ein wie unbegreifliches Genie wird hier verlangt, das neu seine Wurzeln in die alten Jahrhunderte treibt oder die alten Jahrhunderte neu erschafft und mit dem allen sich nicht ausgibt, sondern jetzt erst sich auszugehen beginnt. (T 878)

[This whole literature is a storming of the border and, if Zionism hadn't got in the way, could have developed into a new secret doctrine, a new Kabbalah. The beginnings are there. But it would take a genius of virtually inconceivable stature to push roots into the old centuries or to create the old centuries anew and not exhaust himself doing it but just be at the outset of dispensing his powers.]

Zionism has somehow transformed Kafka's vision of literature, perhaps pulling it away from a kabbalistic esotericism toward a more public mode. Naturally (and justifiably) he doubts that he is suited to the task of linking the "old centuries" to the present. But what is interesting and important is that Kafka connects public and private, a national cause to his opaque way of writing.

Along with Bloom, both Robertson and Suchoff attribute special importance to this passage. Robertson sees in it the suggestion of Kafka's reluctant willingness to become a literary leader of his generation. In support of his contention, Robertson explores an episode of autumn 1922, not long after Kafka abandoned his *Schloß* manuscript. The actual leader of Kafka's generation of German Jewish writers in Prague was Franz Werfel, whose writing Kafka honestly and openly admired (Binder 1966; Pasley 1989). Werfel's effusive, wordy style is diametrically opposed to Kafka's austere reserve, just as his plump body was the opposite of the vegetarian Kafka's hunger-artist physique. Kafka evidently prized the unself-conscious spontaneity of Werfel's prose and poetry. Kafka was warmly open to ways of writing other than his own. However, Werfel's drama *Schweiger* elicited from him a bitterly critical response. Kafka had hoped that he would not have to discuss it with his friend Werfel. Unluckily, Werfel paid a call on Kafka, his friend and fellow writer, that December because the latter was ill. Since Werfel knew that Kafka had read the play, the discussion inevitably turned to *Schweiger*. Kafka did not hold back his critique, and their meeting resulted in an unpleasant scene, hurt feelings on Werfel's part, and feelings of guilt on Kafka's.

Kafka reported the incident in a letter to Brod (MBFK 2:422–23) and he wrote at least two drafts of an apologetic yet still sharply critical letter to Werfel (B 424–25; NS2:526–30). In all these letters — their number alone suggests how troubled he was over the matter — Kafka asserts that the play disgusted him. It deals with the social and political problems facing Kafka's generation in Prague. Werfel, says Kafka, failed to face these problems squarely, preferring instead to divert his plot into the socially and politically empty dead-end of psychoanalysis. For Kafka, whose aversion to psychoanalytic language and theory is well documented, Werfel's drama amounts to moral cowardice.

In the draft of the letter to Werfel that Robertson discusses, Kafka flatters Werfel's wounded ego, calling him a "Führer der Generation," leader of the generation, which Werfel — the most prolific and commercially successful of all Kafka's circle — surely was. But what Kafka gives with one hand he takes back with the other, saying that it is not much of a generation to be the leader of. Still, Werfel has that role, and the play betrays that leadership, Kafka wrote, by reducing their generation's spiritual torment to a psychoanalytic anecdote, the story of a man who happens to have a mental problem.

Robertson, via a circuitous and speculative set of references, takes Kafka's phrasing, "Führer der Generation," to mean more than meets the eye. According to him it is supposed to be an allusion to the Hasidic tradition. Since Kafka had been studying Hebrew since 1917, Robertson refers the expression to the Hebrew *rosh ha-dor*, which means the same thing. And the phrase *rosh ha-dor*, Robertson tells us, is "much used by the Ba'al Shem," the eighteenth-century founder of Hasidism. The Ba'al Shem, says Robertson (citing Scholem), is a man living with God who uses his power to draw his fellow man upward. Since Kafka wrote some Hasidic tales into his diary in 1915, and since he might have known others, Robertson surmises that Kafka must also have known about the *tsaddik*, a figure who appears once every hundred years to exercise spiritual power in secret.

> In the early eighteenth-century the *tsaddik ha-dor*, contemporary with the Ba'al Shem, was an ordinary merchant living in the Galician town of Drohobycz. Kafka also knew about the *Lamed Vov*, the thirty-six just men in every generation on whom the world reposes, even though no-one is permitted to know who they are. In these figures, who carried out their spiritual tasks in complete obscurity, Kafka found his own role as a responsible writer. (1985:224)

Robertson puts more pressure on Kafka's diction than it will bear. The more reasonable explanation of Kafka's phrasing is that he simply meant what he said without making exotic allusions that Werfel would not have understood anyway. If there is an allusion at all, it is probably to the play.

Schweiger himself is supposed to be a Führer-type, sought after by the social democrats of the plot because of his charisma (Werfel 1959:333). But Robertson has made the detour for a specific reason. He is trying to argue that Werfel's intellectual abdication forced Kafka to see himself, reluctantly, as the "Führer der Generation." This, of course, is the same Kafka who some years earlier doubted that he had anything at all in common with the Jewish community: "What do I have in common with the Jews? I hardly have anything in common with myself and ought just stand quietly in a corner, satisfied that I can breathe" (T 622). That was in 1914. By 1922 not much had changed.

When Martin Buber decided to give up editing his monthly journal of Jewish affairs, *Der Jude*, Felix Weltsch hoped Kafka might be interested in taking over, though Kafka's name evidently did not come into serious consideration (Brod, Rosenzweig, and Weltsch seem to have been the primary contenders). The idea that anyone might have tossed his hat into the ring struck Kafka as silly:

> Was mich betrifft, ist es leider nur Spaß oder Halb-Schlaf-Einfall bei der Vakanz des "Juden" an mich zu denken. Wie dürfte ich bei meiner grenzenlosen Unkenntnis der Dinge, völligen Beziehungslosigkeit zu Menschen, bei dem Mangel jedes festen jüdischen Bodens unter den Füßen an etwas derartiges denken? Nein, nein. (MBFK 2:402)

> [As for me, sadly, it can only be a joke or the kind of idea that might come to you in a doze, to think that I might fill the vacancy at *Der Jude*. How could I, with my boundless ignorance of these things, my complete lack of relation to human beings, the utter absence of any solid Jewish ground beneath my feet even consider such a thing? No, no.)

These are not the words of a man willing to consider himself the leader of his generation, even in a pinch. If Kafka had had thoughts about intellectual or spiritual leadership at all, he would have at least been flattered at the prospect of stepping into such a prestigious and meaningful role. His renunciation of leadership is unequivocal.

Even if we accept Robertson's assumption that Kafka's wording is not just rhetoric to flatter Werfel's wounded pride ("Führer der Generation" occurs only in the one draft that Robertson comments on), it does not necessarily follow that Kafka thought it his own task to become a Führer. Judging from Kafka's own meticulously, even ruthlessly, honest writings, his task as writer was simply to represent the

misery of his generation with brave clarity, not to take up the mantel of
messianic leadership. Kafka saw no way out for himself or for his generation, no possibility of redemption, no cure for the spiritual malaise.

Robertson's claim that Kafka saw himself as a leader of his generation in his last years does not persuade for yet other reasons. First, Kafka knew he was dying man. He instructed Max Brod to destroy his
letters, manuscripts, and even the published works he might be able to
lay hands on. This is not the last will and testament of an aspiring
leader. Second, Kafka had only recently been defeated by yet another
major writing project, *Das Schloß*. The works he did complete do not
offer any serious contenders for the role of pointing the way to the
promised land. Third, literature does not work in secret. It has to be
published, brought to the public's attention, read and discussed. There
is nothing to suggest that Kafka thought he was writing for some secret coterie of spiritual legislators. The cryptic passage about his work
as a potential Kabbalah suggests the priority of the category of public.
The esoteric doctrine did *not* come to be, writes Kafka, precisely because Zionism, the public issue, changed the direction of his imaginative life, giving it a more public cast.

Suchoff's essay helps to limn the public — that is, Jewish and possibly even culturally "Zionist" — dimension of *Das Schloß*. In a strategy similar to Robertson's, Suchoff also anchors his argument in a
public literary issue, turning not to Werfel but to Brod. In 1909 Brod
had published a novella called *Ein tschechisches Dienstmädchen* (A
Czech Chambermaid), for which he was widely attacked. It is the story
of an interethnic affair between a Czech maid named Pepi and a
young, assimilated German Jew from Vienna. The Czech readership
objected to Brod's figuration of Czech identity as a helpless domestic
in need of a German-Jewish man to lead her. Austrian Germans
thought the book pro-Czech, rife with dangerously nationalistic un-
dertones. And Jews objected to the portrayal of the protagonist, William Schurhaft, as a demeaning stereotype: the young urban Jew so
alienated from his ethnicity that his Jewishness passes unnoticed. Even
his name is alienated. Finally, the reconciliation between peoples, symbolized in the erotic union of William and Pepi, struck everybody as
phony. For Brod personally, the criticism was a turning point. It awak-
ened in him a reflective sense of his Jewishness in the nationalistically
tense times of prewar Bohemia.

Suchoff does not insist that the story directly influenced Kafka's
plan for *Das Schloß*, though it might have. There are modest parallels.
William searches for Pepi down in the maid's quarters, much as K. is

later invited by the castle's Pepi to join her down below in the maid's quarters (which in Kafka has the rather spookier connotations of a sex crypt). Pepi has an erotic liaison with K. in mind. Suchoff does not insist on the resemblance. Instead, he draws attention to the larger issue of the sexual rhetoric of Brod's allegory. He sensibly proposes that it shows the convergence of sex, class, nationality, and ethnicity was a familiar story in Kafka's Prague. Prague's Jewish readers and their Czech neighbors would have been capable of recognizing erotic relations as symbols for political and national struggle (Suchoff 1994:166). Indeed, by the early twentieth century the interpenetration of sexuality and nationalism was well established in European public consciousness (Mosse 1985). The specific historical moment in Prague, after the founding of the Republic of Czechoslovakia, was one of intense friction between Czechs, Germans, and Jews.

For Kafka this was not a theoretical question. During the period in which he began writing *Das Schloß*, he was having an anxiety-ridden, sexually conflicted affair with a Czech Catholic woman, Milena Jesenská, whose family roots ran deep in Czech history. Kafka became interested in her while he was still engaged to Julie Wohryzek and Milena was living in Vienna with her Jewish husband. During the anti-Semitic riots that broke out in Prague in November 1920, Kafka wrote to her that the hatred directed against Jews washed over him every day:

> Die ganzen Nachmittage bin ich jetzt auf den Gassen und bade im Judenhaß. "Prašivé plameno" habe ich jetzt einmal die Juden nennen hören. Ist es nicht das Selbstverständliche [*sic*], daß man von dort weggeht, wo man so gehaßt wird (Zionismus oder Volksgefühl ist dafür gar nicht nötig)? Das Heldentum, das darin besteht doch zu bleiben, ist jenes der Schaben, die auch nicht aus dem Badezimmer auszurotten sind. (M 288)

> [During entire afternoons I am out on the streets bathing in hatred directed against the Jews. I've now once heard Jews called "the mangy race." Isn't it self-evident that you just leave a place where they hate you so much (Zionism and national pride are not prerequisites)? The heroism of staying in spite of it all is the heroism of cockroaches in the bathroom that can't be exterminated.]

The Jewish self-hatred that wells up in the last lines is a stain that darkens his letters to Milena. But even his self-hatred was divided. He was sometimes disgusted with himself for being what he thought of as a typically alienated Western Jew. In his relationship with Milena the stereotype also included a supposedly predatory lust of Jewish men for

Gentile women (M 68). But his sense of guilt fluctuated. He was more often disgusted with himself for not being Jewish enough — a proud Zionist, a speaker of Hebrew, the father of Jewish children (Binder 1979:476–84).

I adduce the affair with Milena here as support for Suchoff's thesis that ethnic tension, national identity, miscegenation, and the false possibility of sexual reconciliation are likely shaping elements of *Das Schloß*. In this connection it should be noted too that Ottla, Kafka's favorite sister, married a Czech Gentile in July 1920. Besides being a Catholic, her husband, Josef David, was a supporter of the conservative nationalist cause. The Kafka family was almost solidly against the match; only Ottla's brother Franz supported her choice. During most of the summer that Kafka was writing *Das Schloß* he stayed with his sister and her husband in their rented vacation cottage in the countryside.

Given the pervasiveness of the sexual-national issue in Kafka's life and times, it would be surprising if some echo of it did not occur in *Das Schloß*. Yet it is difficult to discern that resonance. Suchoff makes a strong case for nationalist underpinnings in the Amalia episode. He hears in it the echoes of Kafka's social and political sympathies. At the same time, he resists the temptation to assign to Amalia a symbolic nationality, even though her pariah status points toward Jewish connotations. For Suchoff, the point is that she refuses to be pinned down — first in Sortini's bed but also as a symbolic figure in the novel. Her ascetic silence, figured in the text as a contrast to the gossipy Pepi and as a refusal to trade in the otherwise ubiquitous *Schloßgeschichten*, the novel's universal currency, calls forth the theme of sexual domination as a way of enforcing social conformity.

Yet in the end Suchoff reads the fire department festival as an event rich in specifically Jewish connotations, positing a kabbalistic indulgence in occluded meanings. That Kafka sets the festival's date on July 3, his own birthday, suggests a system of private meanings may be in play. Suchoff does not intend to reduce *Das Schloß* to coded autobiography, but he does draw freely on the possibility, indeed the likelihood, that personal elements helped form the book. Amalia's rebellion against the castle is simultaneously a rebellion against her father, a villager fully assimilated to the castle's authority. The grotesquely comic sexual imagery — the all-male volunteer fire department's childish glee over its new fire pump (fitted with its phallic nozzle, the "Spritze") — stands for the authority of the castle and the conformism of the father, an officer in the fire department.

Suchoff ties the fire department scene to a dream Kafka had in 1911. He also follows Hartmut Binder's suggestion that the fire engine material came from an allegorical frieze on a building Kafka knew. Neither connection is impossible, but they seem less than conclusive. More compelling is Suchoff's observation that the popular ritual of the festival enforces the bond between the castle and the village. The demand that the village sacrifice its virgin daughters to the appetites of castle bureaucrats reveals that solidarity for what it really is: mass abasement. That no one except Amalia sees the primitive mating ritual for what it is only emphasizes the completeness of the conformism.

In the trumpet blasts of the festival, Suchoff hears the martial shofars, the ram's-horn trumpets of the Hebrew Bible, heralding Amalia's one-woman uprising. In Isaiah 27:13, for example, the ritual trumpets sound a call to the Israelites to take up arms against the enemy. In *Das Schloß* only Amalia heeds the archaic call, and if Suchoff is right in his claim that the assertion of ethnic identity informs her act of defiance, then Amalia is certainly the tale's preeminently subversive figure in Kafka's new Kabbalah. However, one wonders at the relation between these carefully concealed allusions and the mass-culture part of Suchoff's argument. Like Robertson, Suchoff relies heavily on amassing whatever historical-critical evidence he can muster in support of his position. He is persuasive in his argument that ethnic and national questions have found their way into the Amalia episode. He connects them to Kafka's earlier enthusiasm for the Yiddish theater, the popular repository for Kafka's feelings of ethnic identity and solidarity. Yet *Das Schloß* is a novel, one that was not written for a popular audience or indeed for any audience at all: "Ich weiß," wrote Kafka to Brod, "daß es doch nur da ist zum Geschrieben – , nicht zum Gelesenwerden" (MBFK 2:389). It was a novel just for the sake of the writing, not meant to be read.

Suchoff makes a persuasive case not because he plies his reader with incontrovertible evidence. Such evidence does not exist. Robertson's archeological dig into Kafka's Judaism and politics has reached a limit beyond which Kafka scholarship will not easily go unless new and unexpected documentation should appear. Apart from the novel's possible but undocumentable origins in Kafka's enthusiasm for Yiddish theater, Hasidic lore, and Jewish folkways in Central Europe, the crucial nexus between *Das Schloß* and mass culture lies, I think, in its status as a modern classic.

In some cases classic and popular overlap. The traditional line between popular culture and high culture has become difficult to uphold

for more than one reason. Suchoff shows that Kafka drew from popular Jewish culture. Other modernist classics of high culture have done
likewise. Kafka's castle novel draws on Jewish popular culture as surely
as Bartók and Janáček drew on popular music for their compositions.
But that does not make any of them "popular" in the sense of mass
culture. Yet there is a sense in which Kafka has become popular in the
sense of contemporary popular culture that has recently been under
attack from the defenders of high culture.

One of the more recent (and most popular) attempts to uphold the
elite status of high culture in art is Allan Bloom's *Closing of the American Mind* (1987). In it Bloom objects that American culture and intellectual life have become trivial through the baleful influence of popular
culture. The scene of the worst ravages are the American university,
expressed in the breakdown of the canon and consensus of the fifties.
He blames the decline on the social transformations that took place
during the sixties and pays special attention to the place in that metamorphosis of ethnic minorities in the university. The flood of women,
blacks, Asians, and other minority groups since the late sixties, each
seeming to vaunt its own agenda and alternative canon, has diluted the
traditional core canon of great books, diverting students' minds into
ephemeral pursuits. What Bloom objects to, at bottom, is the democratization of the university, which has supposedly led to a crisis in liberal education. After the Second World War, American and European
universities became progressively more accessible to a broader spectrum of the population. The GI Bill, the National Defense Education
Act, and, a little later, civil rights legislation led to a demographic shift
in higher education that changed the student body and eventually the
faculty (Lauter 1991). The new admission policies meant more
women, more ethnic minorities, and consequently a less homogeneous
student body and, eventually, faculty. The university has become a
more "popular" institution than at any earlier time.

There can be little doubt that the canon of European classics has
had a blind spot in the areas of class, gender, and race. However, the
skeptical outlook advocated by many postsixties critics does not necessarily mean, as Bloom has supposed (rising up against the most ex-
treme opposing views that presented themselves on the horizon) that
the classics must be eliminated in order to make way for whatever texts
may be conducive to the short-term social goals of certain critics. Instead it means that classic texts — *Das Schloß*, for example — are ready
to be read in new ways. The democratization of the university and of
literary criticism as a practice and profession means that scholars and

students from more diverse backgrounds than ever before are reading such classics.

Gloomily, Bloom has asserted that these changes will result in the collapse of the serious study of classic works of literature (Bloom 1991). However, the fate of *Das Schloß* as a classic novel suggests that the opposite is true. It is read by literally masses of students and continues to inspire a massive secondary literature. That Kafka did not write it for an audience is beside the point because the book, once in the mills of the publishing industry and the postwar university, has become popular. Even the nature of its material production points to mass culture. It is readily available in inexpensive, mass-produced editions in various languages. And while it may not outsell the latest thriller or romance topping the current best-seller charts, it will outsell them in the long run. The publishers know this. Kafka's fiction is readily available not because of trade publishers' altruistic commitment to high culture but because Kafka is more popular than the writers who sell for a few years and are then replaced and forgotten.

But perhaps the most relevant aspect of the popular standing of *Das Schloß* is its ability to sustain a dialogue with its readers. Consider the urgency and clarity with which Kafka and *Das Schloß* spoke during the sixties to Czechs and Slovaks of the Prague Spring, when the two great culture heroes of the day were Frank Zappa and Franz Kafka. Obviously the historical and political setting shaped the response of figures like Milan Kundera and Ivan Klíma (the latter even adapted *Das Schloß* for the stage [1971]), but that in no way undermines the power of the novel. On the contrary, it enhances it as a source of insight and solidarity for its admirers and also as a subversive threat to its detractors. Similarly, the Cold War conditioned responses to *Das Schloß* in the United States and Western Europe. The novel spoke first of all about the critics' immediate world, not Kafka's.

In the eighties and nineties the conditioning circumstance of studies like Robertson's, Heidsieck's, and especially Suchoff's and Harold Bloom's is the rise of multiculturalism as a public and intellectual issue, not least in the American Jewish community, though not there alone. The rediscovery of ethnic identity in countries supporting large and ethnically diverse communities — such as France, the United Kingdom, the United States, and the Federal Republic of Germany — has finally led to a literary exploration of the complexly ramified links between ethnic culture and the dominant literary tradition. Kafka is now being presented as a harbinger of this movement. He did not have that Nietzschean contempt for "the herd" that is supposedly common among many modernists, especially those inclined toward reactionary politics. Kafka neither exaggerated nor denied the simple fact that culture and society are intertwined.

The most recent trend of Kafka criticism toward the exploration of this relationship is sensible and justifiable, as Robertson, Suchoff, Bloom, Alter and many others have shown. Moreover, it may be leading gradually in the direction of a redefinition of what modernism was. Literary modernism has traditionally been regarded as a bastion of erudite and forbidding artwork, literature for the elite few, not the unwashed many. The leading theorist of modernism as defined from the perspective of its difficulty and autonomy is Theodor Adorno. Adorno identified popular culture largely with the manipulations of the culture industry, a connection that by now is too obvious to challenge.

What television viewer of the current generation of academic critics, born in the fifties, will ever forget that *The Beverly Hillbillies* was sponsored by a tobacco conglomerate whose slogan was "Winston tastes good, like a [clack, clack] cigarette should"? Nor can the accompanying jingle be expunged from memory. But high art, too, as the post-Adorno generation has come to accept, is commercially manipulable. Andy Warhol was the most brazen marketeer of upscale artwork for the very rich and very hip. The art market as a whole in New York City is the most conspicuous example, as a look through the pages of any chic art journal will show. High art is big business. Even Kafka has not escaped commodification. He may not rank as high as Elvis Presley or Marilyn Monroe on the index of culture icons, but he has made a strong showing. Kafka T-shirts, postcards, and wall posters are not oddities around college campuses and bookstores. Elvis and Kafka exist there on an equal footing.

Moreover, there is also action on the high end of the scale. When the manuscript of *Der Proceß* went on the block at Sotheby's in 1988, it sold for a stunning $1.98 million dollars, just as any van Gogh or famous Picasso might. The manuscript's seller, no doubt, had been speculating on its value for a long time, as any other art investor might.

The interrelations among high art, commerce, aesthetic autonomy, and popular culture are complex. Closer discriminations are called for than those Adorno was willing to make. His notorious incomprehension of jazz, for example, has been widely remarked. He lacked the interest and ability to discriminate between its various forms, its gradations and degradations. Blues and jazz, from Robert Johnson to Cecil Taylor, have always been subversive to one degree or another, both as an expression of black suffering and defiance, and as a specifically aesthetic point of orientation for the assertion of black identity.

The notions of authenticity attendant on blues and jazz as a unique (that is, autonomous, in the sense promoted by Adorno himself) assertion of blackness conform to the traditionally German preoccupation with discovering or forming an authentic self. Though the differences are many, there is good reason to apply Kafka's commentary about Josefine's relationship with her community to figures such as, say, Bessie Smith or Ma Rainey.

> Bei ihren Koncerten besonders in ernster Zeit haben nur wenige Interesse an der Sängerin als solcher, . . . die eigentliche Menge hat sich — das ist deutlich zu erkennen — auf sich selbst zurückgezogen. Hier in den dürftigen Pausen zwischen den Kämpfen träumt das Volk, es ist als lösten sich dem Einzelnen die Glieder, als dürfte sich der Ruhelose einmal nach seiner Lust im großen warmen Bett des Volkes dehnen und strecken. Und in diese Träume klingt hie und da Josefinens Pfeifen; sie nennt es perlend; wir nennen es stoßend; aber jedenfalls ist es hier an seinem Platze, wie nirgends sonst, wie Musik kaum jemals den auf sie wartenden Augenblick findet. Etwas von der armen kurzen Kindheit ist darin, etwas von verlorenem, nie wieder aufzufindenem Glück, aber auch etwas vom tätigen heutigen Leben ist darin, von seiner kleinen unbegreiflichen und dennoch bestehenden und nicht zu ertötenden Munterkeit. (NS2:667–68)

> [At her concerts, especially in difficult times, few have an interest in the songstress as such . . . . The actual masses — it is plain to see — are thrown back on themselves. Here in the moments of respite between struggles the people dream. It is as if the individual were to relax his limbs, as if he, otherwise in ceaseless motion, were permitted to stretch himself out in the great, warm bed of the people. And into these dreams Josephine's piping sounds here and there. She calls it pearl-like; we call it racket. In any case, it is in its proper place here as nowhere else, as music almost never finds the moment that awaits it. Something of our poor, short childhood is in it, something of the irretrieveably lost happiness; but also something of today's busy life is there, of its small, incomprehensible, and yet resolute and unsinkable good cheer.]

The passage, which reads like a description of the blues, gives Kafka's most affirmative view of art. The song is liberating, not just for the few but for the many. Without becoming redemptive figures themselves, Josephine and the blues women manage to offer, fleetingly, just a little bit of the saving force of art, what the Frankfurt theorists, following

Stendhal, liked to call its *promesse de bonheur*. Of course it is true that the art of American singers can be compromised by commercial interests in ways that Josefine's cannot. But the comparison is not a fair one. After all, Josefine and the mouse-folk are imaginary, which is a considerable advantage. Only in the ideal space of the imagination can art be absolutely beyond commerce.

From a historical point of view, the rise of black jazz coincides with the rise of modernism and arguably is a unique expression of the modernist imagination. Nevertheless, jazz has seldom been taken seriously as a form of modernism because it is a popular rather than a high-culture phenomenon. There are signs that this is changing. In contemporary American drama, autonomous features of the black experience, especially blues and jazz, are being explored in the works of Angus Wilson.

The question that David Suchoff poses in his book about the modern novel, which culminates with his study of *Das Schloß*, circles around the issue of popular versus high culture. Though he relies on Adorno's style of cultural criticism in many other ways, he does not follow Adorno on this point. For Adorno, mass culture is fully compromised by the culture industry. Suchoff seeks finer discrimination, seeking to break down the distinction between high and low culture by showing the elements of popular Jewish culture that went into the making of *Das Schloß*.

It seems to me that there are other signs pointing toward Kafka's place in popular culture. Not least among them is Kafka's status in contemporary popular culture. According to the immensely popular best-seller *Cultural Literacy* by E. D. Hirsch Jr., Kafka is a matter of popular knowledge (Hirsch 1988:182). The word *kafkaesque* has become a permanent feature of the language, and not just among literary highbrows. In addition, Kafka himself is something of a cultural icon. Think of his place in the most popular works of Philip Roth (*The Breast*, for example, Roth's affectionate send-up of "Die Verwandlung") or in the comic films and comedy routines of Woody Allen, in which Kafka is a frequent and characteristic point of reference for the Allen persona.

That Kafka has made it into the movies, certainly the most characteristic aesthetic mode of popular culture, is perhaps most decisive. Classic works of fiction in an academic setting, especially in the "great works" format of instruction, can take on aspects of a cultural commodity. Woody Allen and Philip Roth can play on Kafka in their work because he is common currency in middle-class American culture. Any college student, or at least the ones who are at all willing to accept literature as a worthy course of study, are likely to agree that you are supposed to have a knowledge of works such as *Das Schloß* in order to be an educated person.

Still, the technological turn from word to image militates against books like *Das Schloß*. Many, perhaps most, contemporary undergraduates take more readily to film than to prose fiction. The reasons for this are plain. Their imaginations are educated by the image technology of screen and television media well before they even learn to read. Film culture is a part of daily life for most, while the reading and rereading of difficult novels is an acquired taste. Still, movies pave the way.

Film versions of Kafka's fiction, such as Orson Welles's *The Trial* (1962) and Rudolf Noelte's *Das Schloß* (1968), can be taken as a confirmation of Kafka's prestige within the realm of popular culture. They can also be understood as a form of commentary. The scene in which Noelte's K., played by Maximilian Schell, pays a call on the village superintendent, who proceeds to search compulsively for a years-old document pertaining to a surveyor once summoned, is fine and funny exploration of the original scene's native comedy. Its relationship to the original is more than simply parasitic because the film explores some of the comic possibilities inherent in Kafka's original.

Still, the films ultimately have more to do with Welles and Schell and film as an autonomous art form than they do with the novel or with Kafka, whose aesthetic culture is emphatically, exclusively, even obsessively the written word. On October 25, 1915, shortly before *Die Verwandlung* was published as an individual volume, Kafka shot off a panicked letter to his publisher, half pleading, half demanding that no drawing of the insect appear on the cover of the book: "Das bitte nicht! . . . Das Insekt selbst kann nicht gezeichnet werden. Es kann aber nicht einmal von der Ferne aus gezeigt werden." Kafka constructed his bug out of nothing but words, and the perspective of his unique style gives the tale an identity that resists the passivity and reductive specificity of visual illustration.

Image radically restructures the aesthetic experience of literature. In *Das Schloß* Kafka leaves his K. undescribed and featureless, an option not open to film. We do not know and are not intended to know what he looks like. But in the movie he looks like a movie star, Maximilian Schell. The handsome leading man's visual presence undoes K.'s featurelessness, and, worse yet, his movie-star charisma works against the unique and highly specific anonymity of the literary figure. The flatness of character that is characteristic of Kafka's fiction works against what postsilent-era film does best, which is to provide a forum for the unfolding of outsize personality. And finally, film adaptation has a permanence and fixity that Kafka's words do not have. Film is a different imaginative experience with its own opportunities and virtues, but it lacks the general flexibility of the Kafkan novel. Film inevitably simplifies the original Kafkan complexities, as when Orson Welles botches the end of *The Trial* by having an apparent anarchist toss down a load of dynamite on top of Josef K. And art film adaptations lean heavily on the cachet of Kafka's fiction as a genuine piece of European intellectual elitism that is above commercial corruption (because it is relatively less profitable at the box office than ordinary movies) and in some respects well suited to cinema, mainly because of its distinctive imagery.

It may be that the movies have the power to drive out competing images, including that of their own source material. Examples abound. Before American children are old enough to read *Moby-Dick*, they are likely to have seen John Huston's film version rerun many times on television. The ones who later come to the novel will probably find their imagination's prerogative has been usurped. In their reading of the book, Melville's Captain Ahab will look and sound just like Gregory Peck. Something of the Hollywood star's clichéd aura will cling retrospectively to the original. There are probably even people for whom, whether they like it or not, Charlton Heston irrepressibly comes to mind when they think of Moses or the Ten Commandments. Nevertheless, the point stands that Kafka has found his way into popular culture.

Movies made from novels, obviously, are not necessarily or always a bad thing. Middling books have been made into cinematically potent works of art (for example, *Schindler's List*). There is no reason that some good books can't also be made into good movies. Still, Kafka has resisted translation into the medium of film, most recently in Steven Soderbergh's *Kafka* (1992), a glitzy commercialization of material skimmed from the surface of the writer's life and fiction. It simplifies themes and motifs popularly associated with Kafka, packaging them for quick consumption in slick, easy-to-digest cinematography, with the added attraction of star actors (Jeremy Irons plays Kafka and is supported by Theresa Russell, Joel Grey, and Alec Guiness). However, the aesthetic weakness of the film is beside the point. More important is the simple fact that Kafka has seeped deep enough into the popular psyche to get into the movies at all.

Let me turn again to the question of popular culture and the question of reimagining modernism. If we are to accept Kafka's work as an exploration of Jewish identity — either because we are persuaded that Kafka wrote it that way intentionally, as Robertson and Suchoff argue, or because it speaks to Jewish concerns regardless of Kafka's specific wishes and intentions, as Harold Bloom believes — then it makes sense to seek comparable literary work in the same period. It may be productive to compare Kafka's sense of minority ethnic status to the way in which it has been dealt with elsewhere.

In his effort to define the nature of black modernism in the United States, Michael Cooke (1984) offers Kafka as the classical and typical European modernist. But he argues that Kafka's modernism is diametrically opposed to the modernism of African-American writers emerging in the same period. Kafka's negative vision of the ethnic self, expressed for Cooke above all in Gregor Samsa's verminous condition, finds no correlate in the literature of inchoate black modernism. Cooke believes that American black literature is a good deal more life-affirming than the world-weary modernism of Europe, of which Kafka's modernism is the prime example. It is unfortunate that Cooke did not take Josefine as his figure of orientation, but he is probably right that Gregor Samsa is more widely perceived as characteristic.

Still, the contrast may not hold. For some years now, since she was belatedly "discovered" in the early seventies, Zora Neale Hurston has played a role in the formation of American black literary culture similar to the one that Kafka is playing in the secular, intellectual perception of modern Jewish identity. Hurston's books epitomize a significant piece of black cultural identity in a way similar to Kafka's role in giving expression to a substantial piece of the modern Jewish experience. In her most influential novel, *Their Eyes Were Watching God* (1937), a decent man turns into a raving, murderous animal. The transformation is not literal like Gregor Samsa's, but it is a metamorphosis from man to beast all the same. Hurston's figure is bitten by a rabid dog and, as the disease takes its course, begins to behave like one and must finally be shot dead. The metaphorical implications of Hurston's vision may not be so different from Kafka's. While no binding generalizations can be made from such a small point of contact, even when the works in which it occurs are of such major importance, the convergence suggests at least that the matter bears further consideration. Hurston's modernism is anchored not in formal experiment but in a deep concern with racial and national origins. It is the search for traditional roots in a disintegrating world, a search for solid foundations that she shares not only with Kafka but also variously with Yeats, Pound, Eliot, Joyce, and Mann.

There is no compelling reason that ethnicity should not figure into a new, enlarged, and redirected definition of literary modernism. Yeats's imagination, for example, is distinctively Irish in its conscious orientation. T. S. Eliot was consciously trying to forge an identity rooted in nation and religion. William Faulkner's modernism hinges on issues of race, sex, and cultural identity. His novels explore the inner tensions of the post-Civil War South that are not in principle different from those of Franz Joseph's moribund Austria-Hungary. Its multicultural unity collapsed under the weight of the same issues that haunted Faulkner's imagination: racism, old families, outdated institutions, a lost war, dying traditions. Similarly, British and French colonial literature are deeply preoccupied with problems of race, sex, and cultural identity. That Kafka overlaps with this larger configuration should not come as a surprise.

6: The Impossibility of Crows

THE TURN OF Kafka studies into cultural criticism has helped to make Kafka more intelligible in two main ways: first, by situating him better than ever before with respect to his own historical, social, and intellectual context, and second, by positioning him with respect to the contemporary interest in race and ethnicity, community and individuality. Even if it remains difficult to translate the specific details of his fiction (imagery, allusion, form) directly into social meanings, his own manifest interest in Judaism, coupled with contemporary critical interest in questions of multiculturalism and social identity, authorizes the approach offered by cultural studies. Still, cultural criticism has its limits. It cannot contain all of Kafka; his fiction remains too subversive. Certain questions slip through the nets of cultural critique.

Why, if Kafka was principally interested in giving imaginative form to his cultural roots, is his fiction so unforthcoming about it? The works rarely refer to Jews or Judaism and its rituals. Moreover, the language of his fiction is purged not only of any hint of Jewish speech but of practically all distinguishing features of class, region, and ethnicity. Even children, barbarians and animals use the same neutral idiom that the adults do. The reason, I think, is that Kafka was interested in achieving in his writing a sense of universal timelessness and placelessness. This is not meant to suggest that the topic of Judaism is excluded from his fiction, only that Kafka meant the fiction to encompass even more. He had an abiding fascination for what might be called the anthropological absolute. By this I mean a piece or level of human reality that inhabits but also transcends the contingencies of institutions such as state and religion and ethnicity.

When Kafka wrote in his diary about "storming the last earthly border" by means of his writing, it certainly sounds as if at least he believed his fiction had some capacity to resist the contingencies of time and circumstance. On December 25, 1917, he wrote that works of his such as "Ein Landarzt" gave him a modicum of satisfaction but that happiness would come only if he succeeding in elevating the world into "the pure, the true, the unchanging." These words disclose his deepest point of artistic departure. There is every indication that Kafka regarded this task as the supreme challenge to his literary gift, even if there is no indication that he thought he ever measured up to it fully. Even Josefine, his most affirmative artist figure, achieves at best an ambiguous success. No one can tell how her "piping" differs from that of any other mouse's. Indeed, it may not be her piping at all that so delights the mouse-folk at her recitals but the "feierliche Stille," the ceremonial silence that envelops and unites them as they listen to her. Josefine's song is an art beyond concept and reference. It is an art that *does* something rather than *saying* something.

Kafka's achievement in *Das Schloß* is in principle similar, as should be evident at this late date in Kafka criticism. It is not so much what he says as the forum that he has provided for discussion, debate, exchange, and disagreement. His book is not an act of communication so much as the scene of it. Early in his career he wrote that we need books that affect us like a sharp blow to the head. *Das Schloß*, historically, has turned to be a blow to our collective heads. It is news that stays news, inexhaustible not because it appeals directly to the emotions — indeed, its undercooled style hardly appeals to emotion at all — but because it appeals to the imagination, the sense of mystery and the sublime. The last category is especially pertinent. *Das Schloß* is deeply concerned with that which lies above and beyond mimetic expression, inspires awe and fear, and is all but lost to K., the prototypically alienated modern. I want to conclude this study of castle criticism by pursuing this last, insufficiently explored aspect of *Das Schloß*.

Kafka's Anthropological Absolute

In September 1917, after Kafka's tuberculosis was diagnosed, he took a leave of absence from his job and went to the northwestern Bohemian village of Zürau (called Siřem in Czech) for a rest cure. He stayed there several months, until April 1918. It is the received view that this sojourn marks a final renewal of Kafka's creativity. He did not turn away from earlier interests so much as he experienced a new and vigorous development in his way of seeing the world. During this period he turned his hand to writing brief parables and aphorisms, literary miniatures that should be regarded as finger exercises in preparation for *Das Schloß*.

In Zürau he read widely, including works by Buber (with little appreciation), Kierkegaard, Tolstoy, and Schopenhauer; he also read in the Hebrew Bible. In his afterword to *Das Schloß*, Max Brod claimed that Kafka's reading of Kierkegaard was decisive for the novel, supplying Kafka with the basic conception of the earthly and divine as incommensurable. This could be true, though no commentary of Kafka's supports

Brod's contention. It seems likely that Kafka's dualism, expressed in many of his aphorisms, was generated out of his own strangely unique resources of creativity and owes little to Kierkegaard or even to Jewish mystical traditions. Kafka was indeed interested in the Jewish myth and folklore, but the evidence (or rather the lack of it) suggests that his actual, specific knowledge was haphazard and limited. What knowledge he did possess has left no clear trail in his fiction and aphorisms. Consequently the critics have been left to speculate. Robertson guesses the aphorisms to have been vitally shaped by the Kabbalah, and he offers an extensive exegesis of them on this basis, yet he produces no objective evidence in support of the conjecture (1985:195ff).

Nevertheless, the emphasis on the Zürau aphorisms as an imaginative achievement central to Kafka's understanding of the world is on target. Apart from any specifically Jewish component, they also belong to an identifiable European tradition, as Richard Gray (1987) has shown. Finally, even if they are not directly inspired by the Kabbalah — and it seems unlikely that Kafka knew much if anything about it — the character of the aphorisms is distinctly kabbalistic (Alter 1993b).

One such element that is decisive for Kafka's writing, the aphorisms as well as *Das Schloß*, is the gnostic-like, kabbalistic distinction between the earthly here-and-now and a transcendent realm. Kafka often calls it "das Geistige," the spiritual, though it has other names. He sets it above and beyond "die sinnliche Welt," or the sense world, a choice of words that suggests that his background in empirical psychology is also in play here. The sense world is loosely identified with evil ("das Böse"), as in the distinction between sensual love and heavenly love but also more abstractly:

> Es gibt nichts anderes als eine geistige Welt; was wir sinnliche Welt nennen ist das Böse in der geistigen und was wir böse nennen ist nur eine Notwendigkeit eines Augenblicks unserer ewigen Entwicklung. (NS2:124, §54)

> [There is nothing other than a spiritual world; what we call the sensuous world is only the evil within the spiritual one, and what we call evil is only a necessity of a moment in our eternal development.]

The rift between the earthly and the transcendent is complete: "Es gibt ein Ziel, aber keinen Weg," a goal but no pathway that leads there. The resemblance between this last aphorism (§26) and K.'s attempts to get into the castle has often been noted but never adequately clarified. It seems to me that the correspondence is important, but in need of deeper exploration.

Kafka's novel presents a world that is divided into two irreconcilable halves, village and castle. Yet to be in the village, in a certain sense, is to be in the castle, as Schwarzer points out to K. Moreover, bureaucratic officials evidently travel back and forth between the castle and the village. This suggests an arrangement rather like that in aphorism §54, in which the spiritual contains, yet also transcends, the sensual. The distinction between the two is an illusion, but one that is inescapable.

Yet we who are marooned in the realm of the senses are not without recourse. Art may have some modest access to the transcendent realm, though not unproblematically. It is the classic problem of language that Kafka addresses in aphorism §57: language can be used only to intimate (*andeutungsweise*) the things of the spiritual world (see above, p. 83). Language and fiction cannot render them mimetically. The language aphorism brings us to the brink of *Das Schloß*, which enacts as parable a dilemma that is cognate.

The danger in relating the aphorisms to *Das Schloß* lies in exaggerating the correspondence of details, especially conceptual ones. What strikes me as crucial is not so much a precise resemblance as a general one, a similarity of structural framework. Moreover, *Das Schloß* is truer to Kafka's radically uncompromising vision than the aphorisms. By Kafkan standards they are surprisingly blunt in the provisional naming of ineffable, unknowable things. Kafka talks about "das Unzerstörbare" (the indestructible) in human nature, refers longingly to paradise, (also indestructible, according to §74), and "das Geistige" (the spiritual). This reliance on conceptual abstraction is new and uncharacteristic for Kafka. His more usual mode is parable and image.

That he may have felt uneasy about this quasi-philosophical style can be inferred from the aphorism about language, which we have already discussed, but which needs further elaboration with a new inflection:

> Die Sprache kann für alles außerhalb der sinnlichen Welt nur andeutungsweise, aber niemals auch nur annähernd vergleichsweise gebraucht werden, da sie entsprechend der sinnlichen Welt nur vom Besitz und seinen Beziehungen handelt. (NS2:59)

> [Language can only be used to intimate things outside the sensory world. It can never be used comparatively, not even approximately, because language in its correspondence to the sensory world deals only with property and its relations.]

This is Kafka's secular reworking of the traditional Jewish Bilderverbot, the biblical prohibition that forbids the depiction of God or paradise. It seems likely there are other points of reference for Kafka as well. The lessons of empirical psychology would have stayed with him, as we have seen, because it persuaded him that the inner life, contra Proust and Joyce, is beyond representation. In the Zürau period, as we have noted, he was reading Kierkegaard, whose distinction between telling and showing may have impressed him. He was also reading Schopenhauer, whose doctrine of representation as it relates to the will bears a family resemblance to Kafka's notion of language and the spiritual. We may reasonably suppose that Kafka's attitude toward representation and the spirit were thus overdetermined. The failure of language is an ancient topos, the ultimate expression of which is in the decalogue. That the ancient Hebrew source was uppermost in Kafka's mind is suggested by the abundance of biblical allusions to paradise, the tree of knowledge, and original sin in his Zürau aphorisms and in the "Er" pieces of 1920.

In addition, the messianic idea — conditioned by Kafka's growing interest in the need for Jewish solidarity and nationhood — was on his mind, as it was on the minds of many Jews, hard-pressed as they were by the worsening of European nationalisms and attendant anti-Semitism. In the May 1921 issue of *Der Jude*, Martin Buber's Jewish monthly, there appeared an essay on Jewish messianism. Its author, Zionist Elfride-Salome Bergel-Gronemann, writes programmatically of the rigorous, traditional Jewish insistence on the absolute otherness of God and Paradise. She is referring to the *Bilderverbot*. Christianity, by contrast, offers earthly consolation to man's sin-battered soul in the form of symbolic images, especially that of Christ crucified, meant to seal the certainty of man's continuity with the divine. Art is thus an earthly resting place for the spirit. It is otherwise in Judaism. Since Jewish redemption has not yet occurred, it remains an indistinct and undefinable prospect, the object of uncertain longing. Therefore, in Judaism the spirit cannot and does not rest in this world. The infinite and absolute must remain infinite and absolute, beyond all earthly representation. The Messiah cannot be compelled into aesthetic form. Any such embodiment is idolatrous falsification.

Even the secret name of God is not to be spoken. This is the taboo that K. breaks when he speaks aloud the name of Count Westwest, for which the horrified schoolmaster rebukes him. This does not mean Count Westwest personifies God; far from it. It only means that the traditional structure of the taboo remains intact, if misapplied, in the degraded world of the castle. Westwest is something more along the order of secular deity, a false god for the benighted villagers.

The point that Bergel-Gronemann insists on is that the messianic event cannot be depicted because it has not occurred. The Jewish tradition presents redemption above all as a task that remains to be completed. The idea that redemption is a task and not a gift of grace also distinguishes Jewish messianism from the Christian version. Christ redeems the worst sinner, no matter how abject. The sinner is passive and must only desire to be redeemed. In the liberal Western tradition of Judaism that Kafka inhabited, it is the task of all Jews to prepare the world for the coming of the Messiah. However, as Bergel-Gronemann explains, he will come only when the preparations are complete — that is, when he is no longer needed. This is a social and political messianism. Interestingly and significantly, Kafka himself is explicit about this in his aphorisms:

> Der Messias wird erst kommen, wenn er nicht mehr nötig sein wird, er wird erst nach seiner Ankunft kommen, er wird nicht am letzten Tag kommen, sondern am allerletzten. (NS2:57)

> [The Messiah will not come until he is no longer needed. He will come only after his arrival. He will come not on the last day, but on the very last day.]

In a more secular vein, the same thought is transposed as follows:

> Der entscheidende Augenblick der menschlichen Entwicklung ist immerwährend. Darum sind die revolutionären geistigen Bewegungen, welche alles frühere für nichtig erklären, im Recht, denn es ist noch nichts geschehn. (NS2:114, §6)

> [The deciding moment of human development is everlasting. That is why the revolutionary spiritual movements that declare null and void all that has gone before them are in the right. For nothing has yet happened.]

The decisive moment is everlasting because the earth is continually being prepared, so to speak, for the coming of the messiah — that is, for a state of perfection that will never be reached. It is for the same reason that K. will never achieve his aim. It cannot be achieved. Crossing over from the realm of suffering, deception, and incompletion into the absolute is not possible:

> Er fühlt sich auf dieser Erde gefangen, ihm ist eng, die Trauer, die Schwäche, die Krankheit, die Wahnvorstellungen der Gefangenen brechen bei ihm aus, kein Trost kann ihn trösten, weil es eben nur Trost ist, zarter kopfschmezender Trost gegenüber der groben Tatsache des Gefangenseins. Fragt man ihn aber, was er eigentlich haben will, kann er nicht antworten, denn er hat — das ist einer seiner stärksten Beweise — keine Vorstellung von der Freiheit.

[He feels himself imprisoned in this world. He feels closed in. The sadness, the weakness, the sickness, the delusion of the imprisoned break out in him. No consolation can comfort him, simply because it is only consolation, the tender headachy consolation versus the brute fact of imprisonment. But if you ask him what he wants, he cannot answer, because — and this is one of his most solid pieces of evidence — he has no idea (*Vorstellung*) of freedom.]

The "he" in this aphorism is not K., since it is a piece from the "Er" collection of 1920. But it may as well be K., for it describes his situation exactly. He knows that he is suffering, that he wants something better than what he has, but does not even know what that something better is. In the aphorism it is given as freedom. In the novel, that something, the object of K.'s vague longing, is left utterly unnamed.

I am suggesting that Kafka's secularized perception of the messianic ideal took an anthropological turn. It is an insight of Kafkan imagination that the individual contains an indestructible element of spirituality, a tiny, imperishable bit of the paradise that was lost and is yet to come, toward which K. falteringly strives.

Der Mensch kann nicht leben ohne ein dauerndes Vertrauen zu etwas Unzerstörbarem in sich, wobei sowohl das Unzerstörbare als auch das Vertrauen ihm dauernd verborgen bleiben können. Eine der Ausdrucksmöglichkeiten dieses Verborgen-Bleibens ist der Glaube an einen persönlichen Gott. (NS2:124, §50)

[The human being cannot live without a lasting trust in something indestructible within himself. Both the indestructible and the trust can remain perpetually hidden from him. One of the possibilities for the expression of the concealment is the faith in a personal God.]

It is a condition of life, then, that the individual have a lasting confidence in the anthropological absolute, even if he is unaware of it. That the indestructible component of human being is simultaneously present to the imagination yet permanently absent to life lived in time and space is evident from the various invocations of biblical paradise in the Zürau aphorisms. This one is characteristic:

Die Vertreibung aus dem Paradies ist in ihrem Hauptteil ewig: Es ist also zwar die Vertreibung aus dem Paradies endgiltig, das Leben in der Welt unausweichlich, die Ewigkeit des Vorganges aber macht es trotzdem möglich, daß wir nicht nur dauernd im Paradies bleiben könnten, sondern tatsächlich dort dauernd sind, gleichgültig ob wir es hier wissen oder nicht. (NS2:127, §64)

[The expulsion from Paradise is, in the main, eternal: So the expulsion from Paradise is final, life in the world ineluctable, yet the eternity of the process makes it nevertheless possible that we not only could remain continuously in Paradise but actually are there continuously, regardless of whether we know it here or not.]

The language problem is evident. No language has a verb tense that expresses eternity, so Kafka must resort to strategies of parody and paradox to intimate the possibility of a moral dimension beyond time and space. Paradise is indestructible, hidden within — not lost at all, just unknown to us. Paradise is continually present, even if we remain estranged from it and unaware of it. I take the aphorism to be understood not as a philosophical truth but as an exploratory expression, one of many, concerning the essential dividedness of human nature, its lack of unity with itself, especially with a higher element that is always emergent yet never finally achieved.

The upshot of such passages — together with many more that could be offered in evidence — is that Kafka senses the presence of an ideal world outside the sensuous realm of time and space. That explains why the spatiality of his metaphors is unstable, sometimes internal (the indestructible), sometimes external ("Paradise"), but always a human universal that eludes conventional representation. It is a way of thinking that has an identifiable messianic tradition regardless of Kafka's intention, and it offers itself as a clue to understanding the peculiarities of *Das Schloß*. However, it would be a mistake to take the aphorisms too literally. Indeed, the categories with which they proceed (the indestructible, Paradise, the spiritual world) are flawed by self-contradiction. Abstract and metaphorical as they are, they offend the commandment forbidding images; they say too much. They transgress against the postreligious *Bilderverbot* by making the absolute contingent, the infinite finite.

Kafka's massive and supremely discreet parable, *Das Schloß*, corrects the error. It does so precisely because it does *not* offer any image that represents the infinite. All indications suggest that the opposite is true: the castle represents falsehood, idolatry, reification as one of the besetting problems of thought and imagination. The castle and its bureaucracy mask the infinite, concealing it behind a veil of quixotic misapprehension.

Error and the Sublime

We turn first to a crucial passage. The image of the castle and its main feature, the tower, is measured in the text against the implied norm of a lost world. In his mind's eye, K. remembers the church tower of his old hometown and judges the castle tower unfavorably by the standard it sets. In so doing, he comes closest to revealing the novel's ineffable center. The church tower soars confidently, youthfully upward. It unfolds its rooftop in a flash of bright red tiles. This catches the eye because it is one of the novel's only patches of color. Then the narrator adds, "ein irdisches Gebäude — was können wir sonst bauen — aber mit höherem Ziel . . . ." Kafka's mode here is negative affirmation. The building is only terrestrial (that is, not spiritual) but its aim is loftier (but not named). K.'s eye and the narrator's language move on to explore the crow-encircled castle tower. It is crumbling, shabby; it even has an "insane" look about it. It shows little sign of spiritual purpose.

The contrast between church tower and castle tower sets Kafka's theme. It is the earthly, which can be named, and something higher, which cannot, but which the church tower intimates. The contrast should help to confirm the view that the castle stands as an emblem for the modern, secular, postreligious era. It is important to note that K. shows no sign of nostalgia for the past. The past is gone; K. has come here to stay, a point about which he is emphatic. Emphatic too is K.'s striving toward an unnamed goal, which we should take to mean a future that is better. This does not make K. a messianic figure, but it does show that the messianic idea is at work in the novel. It is the idea of a fallen world in need of redemption, but not a redeemer in the form of a personal deity. K. is just an ordinary uprooted soul, aggressively seeking something he wants and needs yet hardly understands and cannot name. He has no clear idea how to fulfill the uncertain longing that drives him forward.

It is reasonable to wonder why Kafka chooses the image of a church rather than a synagogue as his point of comparison. The sense of it has to do with what might be called, orienting our perspective on the novel from the aphorisms, Kafka's anthropological absolute. The aphorisms deal not with the interests and spiritual problems of Jews alone, even though Kafka's own Jewishness certainly helped to shape his perception of basic human nature. When he talks about what is indestructible in people, he means all people, not just Jews. The church in *Das Schloß* refers to the average run of European reality, which is Gentile. If Kafka had added a synagogue, or used one instead of a church, it would have created confusion by giving the false impression that he is writing about the special problems of European Jews. The novel is about the human spirit in the postreligious era of the European mind.

Kafka's clues to this effect are plain enough. The castle tower is residential, not ecclesiastical. The village has no church, only an insignificant little chapel, suggesting the merest vestigial remnants of a once mighty but now defunct religious tradition. In the village the usual stock figures are present: schoolmaster, innkeeper, peasants, and so forth; but there is no priest, pastor, or rabbi. The role of spiritual leader, though still an official presence in *Der Proceß*, has simply disappeared from the world of the castle. K. himself could be a Jew, as his pariah status suggests, and the same holds true for the Barnabassian clan. As Suchoff and Robertson have shown, various elements of Judaism figure into Kafka's imaginary world.

Still, I believe the point is this: Kafka imagines a syncretic setting in which spiritual beliefs and practices have withered into senseless and oppressive parodies of spiritual observance. Religious leadership has been supplanted by a secularized caste of officials who parody the responsibilities and prerogatives of traditional spiritual leaders. And K. himself epitomizes the homeless, faceless, rootless stranger — Jew, Gentile, or anybody — in search of a sense of orientation. He will not find it because he does not know how or where to look. In orienting himself on Klamm (whose name, as noted earlier, means "delusion" in Czech), K. deceives himself. Klamm is the mere semblance of a godlike or priestlike figure, an illusion that K. shares with the villagers, who are in awe of him.

The castle itself is ugly and run-down, in fact not a castle at all but a huddle of low buildings surrounding a tower. The absence of beauty is conspicuous and significant. The castle lacks the symbolic power that is associated with beauty in the sense of the European Christian tradition of symbolization. K. actually dwells on this point in the passage in which he compares the church tower of his hometown to the castle tower. Back home, he recalls, the church tower rose confidently upward, seeming to become more youthful as it did so and then finishing with a flourish of red-tiled rooftop. K. remembers that it had a "loftier purpose" than the secular buildings around it, and he notes that the castle is quite different. It calls forth no sense of a superior purpose. K. notes too that the church tower was just an "earthly building" yet justly laid claim to its higher, spiritual identity. The church tower has symbolic power for K. because it compels into material form an intimation of a spirituality that is beyond the mere material. The castle,

squat and dilapidated, does the opposite. It blocks spirituality, the fulfillment of self and of community.

Kafka presents a world in which beauty is absent. The beautiful
symbolized the continuity of the earthly and the divine. The classic
aesthetic expression of this continuity in European culture is the Roman Catholic tradition of ecclesiastical art, and its ultimate doctrine is
that of transubstantiation. God's divine plan guarantees the coherence
of the universe, and beauty is the visible sign of transcendence, guaran-
tor of continuity between the earthly and the divine. K.'s ugly, snow-
frozen world is one in which transcendence is impossible. The line of
contact between this world and the fuller one that lies deeper has been
broken. The castle, with its jagged battlements, "as if drawn by someone who is frightened or by a child's hand," is the allegory of the failed
transcendence.

The castle and its somnolent army of bureaucrats are Kafka's comic
image for the diminished state of modern spirituality. This is a confirmation and expansion of Ingeborg Henel's fundamental insight that the
castle is a projected counterworld to the protagonist (Henel 1967:259–
69). But whereas Henel refers the counterworld only to the protagonist,
it seems to me that it should be referred to all the other villagers as well.
It is the displaced embodiment of the human frailties of everyone, but
especially K. It reflects not the true human spirit, which I am calling
Kafka's anthropological absolute, but its reified simulacrum.

The castle and its bureaucrats, whose grotesque and comic aspect is
not often enough chuckled over by Kafka critics, reflect the frozen
spiritual lives of K. and the villagers. The bureaucrats — Klamm,
Sortini, Sordini, Erlanger, Galater, Bürgel, and the rest — satirize
bourgeois power and respectability extrapolated to the nth degree.
They stand for the spirit congealed into static, stolid, false forms. The
castle and its grotesque, bureaucratic apparatus are not symbols that
reach outward toward transcendence. They are instead emblems of the
blockage that prevent K. and the villagers from finding a way out of
the eternal winter of the soul that imprisons them. Olga's nightly degradations and Barnabas's futile activities as a courier are telling examples of the castle's falsity. That both of them willingly undertake these
activities suggests that their misery may well be self-imposed. The castle never demanded absolution from Amalia's family (S 328–29).

This view of the castle does not return us to long-discredited religious interpretations of *Das Schloß*. Brod sought to recover Kafka for a
conventional Judaism, and writers such as Ong (1947) and Muir
(1930) and, more recently, Jens and Küng (1985) have sought to

bring Kafka into a position compatible with ecumenical Christian theology. More persuasive are perhaps Harold Bloom (1987) and his precursor Gerschom Scholem, who have explored what they regard as Kafka's spontaneous reinvention of Jewish mysticism. But I would like to suggest, building on Ingeborg Henel's reading of Kafka as a thinker (1980) and in partial agreement with Ritchie Robertson (1985), that Kafka's sense of spirituality has a secular cast, distant from traditional religious dogma and doctrine, distant even from theism itself.[1] Robertson rightly and persuasively identifies Kafka's spirituality not with the supernatural but with the "collective being of mankind united in 'das Unzerstörbare'" (201) and adduces this aphorism:

> Das Unzerstörbare ist eines; jeder einzelne Mensch ist es und gleichzeitig is es allen gemeinsam, daher die beispiellos untrennbare Verbindung der Menschen.

> [The indestructible is whole; it is every individual human being and at the same time all collectively, therefore the unexampled indivisible solidarity of the human race.]

---

[1] I am skeptical about Robertson's view that K. is best understood as a messiah figure, false or not, and that *Das Schloß* is a critique of messianism. I will be arguing that Jewish messianism and the Jewish tradition of not depicting God and Paradise are decisive for the novel and that both are tied to Kafka's utopian belief in a last, indestructible core of pure humanity that inheres in and transcends each individual. The common core is an anthropological universal that, for Kafka at least, accounts for the possibility (but not the achieved actuality, for it is at all times only emergent, never realized) of human community. This everlasting state of incompletion, modeled on the Jewish messianic ideal, is the foundation of Kafka's humane pessimism. Indeed, Kafka's vision of human nature is as pessimistic as the one Freud develops in *Civilization and its Discontents*, but on different grounds. Freud sees reason and instinct locked in perpetual, irreconcilable conflict. It is reason's task to hold rapacious instinct in check so as to make civilized life possible. At first glance Kafka's dualism (the spiritual versus the sensory world) seems parallel. But Kafka's opposition is actually quite different from Freud's. Like Freud, Kafka sees human nature in a state of irreconcilable conflict. But Freud offers instinct as the core of human nature, the source of evil that must be overcome by the exercise of reason. Kafka more optimistically offers a core of indestructible goodness as the basis of human nature. It is a state of spiritual innocence from which we have fallen yet which still exists in us, a condition that remains permanently desired though permanently out of reach. Reason and the senses want to recover this lost state of bliss but cannot because, belonging to this world, they are intrinsically flawed. Reason degenerates inevitably into self-serving connivance, and the senses give themselves over to self-indulgence. K. embodies both failures.

By intellectual disposition and by his training in empirical psychology, Kafka is closer to the antidogmatic pragmatism of William James's *Varieties of Religious Experience: A Study in Human Nature* (1902) than to the theological minds that have claimed him as a kindred spirit. The notion of spirituality adumbrated in Kafka's aphorisms and more subtly and fully explored in *Das Schloß* has more to do with his sense of human nature than with the dogmas of temporal religious institutions. The image of castle and its bureaucracy, as I have been arguing, represents a final institutional petrification of the human spirit in Europe and nearly its death sentence. The aphorisms make it clear that Kafka had not entirely given up on the human spirit, that he sought a sign of something ahistorical and noncontingent, something that might elude the Midas touch of official codification in religion and even in literature and art.

Naturally there are traces of familiar religion, and one seems to me particularly important. The specifically Jewish component of Kafka's sober mysticism links his writing to the perdurable tradition of the sublime. Its decisive component is the Mosaic *Bilderverbot*, the biblical prohibition that underlies Kafkan negation, his endlessly refined tactic of not-naming. In Kafka, the infinite and absolute remain infinite and absolute.

For example, in comparing the church tower to the castle tower, Kafka's K.-like narrative voice talks about the church tower's loftier purpose, but without naming that purpose. And, as Ritchie Robertson shrewdly observes, a similar strategy informs the strange and obscurely metaphorical passage that describes the castle tower (Robertson 1985:203–4). It is "mercifully hidden" by ivy, which has the effect of calling forth feelings that a taboo is being transgressed here, that something better left unseen has greeted the light of day. That hidden something remains unsaid. It evokes in his readers a feeling of the Kafkan sublime. The effect is parallel to Josefine's song. The text does not tell us something. Rather, it causes us to sense the presence of an occulted reality, something uncanny, beyond the threshold of ordinary experience.

The link between the sublime and the *Bilderverbot* is strong. "Perhaps the most sublime passage in the Jewish Law," writes Kant in his *Critique of Judgment*, "is the commandment: Thou shalt not make unto thee any graven image, or any likeness of any thing that is in heaven or on earth, etc. This commandment . . . holds also for our presentation of the moral law, and for the predisposition within us for morality" (1790:135). Kafka has no theory of the sublime, only its experience, which in *Das Schloß* is largely but not entirely blocked by the castle and its obfuscatory bureaucracy. The traces of this momentary experience in his fiction and aphorisms, occasionally figured conceptually (as in his notion of the indestructible within man), offer themselves as an Archimedean point from which to view *Das Schloß*.

Let us look first at light imagery, which is paradigmatic for the sublime. The defining passage in this instance occurs not in *Das Schloß* but in *Der Proceß*. In the parable of the man from the country, who waits a lifetime at the open door of the law yet never musters the courage to enter, light is the crucial image. Just before he dies, at a time when his eyesight is failing (the waning of the bodily senses points toward a waxing of the spiritual one), a radiance (*Glanz*) breaks forth inextinguishably (*unverlöschlich*) through the door of the law. It is the sublime epiphany of the unnameable, indestructible happiness that awaited the man. If we are justified in taking the aphorisms as a guide to the parable, then the fact that the light is inextinguishable is of central importance, pointing toward the undiscovered radiance that was simultaneously within the man (a finite being) but also transcends him as a common property, "the law" of human nature. While the man's life can be extinguished, the light in us all cannot.

As various critics have noted, K. bears some resemblance to the man from the country. We should not bear down on the analogy, however, because K. tries with all his ingenuity to penetrate the castle, whereas the man sits by the open door, not daring to enter. The man from the country is more like Amalia's father. After his daughter's insolent rebellion, he stations himself on the road to the castle begging for absolution for his family, never daring to think that they do not need any, even though castle officials repeatedly tell him they know of no offense. Nevertheless, there is some structural similarity between K.'s castle and "the law" of the man in the parable. The castle and the law function to obstruct passage. The sublime moment comes when the obstruction is momentarily pierced by the light.

In *Das Schloß* the light imagery is just as crucial but more ambiguously subtle. As K. stands eyeing the castle, its weird aspects come into view:

> Der Turm hier oben — es war der einzige sichtbare — , der Turm eines Wohnhauses wie sich jetzt zeigte, vielleicht des Hauptschlosses, war ein einförmiger Rundbau, zum Teil gnädig von Epheu verdeckt, mit kleinen Fenstern, die jetzt in der Sonne aufstrahlten — etwas Irrsinniges hatte das — und einem söllerartigen Abschluß, dessen Mauerzinnen unsicher, unregelmäßig, brüchig wie von ängstlicher oder nachlässiger Kinderhand gezeichnet sich in den blauen Himmel

zackten. Es war wie wenn irgendein trübseliger Hausbewohner, der gerechter Weise im entlegensten Zimmer des Hauses sich hätte eingesperrt halten sollen, das Dach durchbrochen und sich erhoben hätte, um sich der Welt zu zeigen.

[The tower up above — it was the only one visible — turned out now to be residential, perhaps the living quarters of the main castle. It was uniformly round, in part mercifully concealed by ivy and with small windows that now glinted in the sun — this had something insane about it — and was surmounted by a garret-like top whose crenelated wall, unsure, irregular, fragile as if drawn by the fearful or careless hand of a child, jutted into the blue sky. It was as if some wretched occupant, who justifiably ought to have kept himself locked up in the most remote room of the house, had broken through the roof and risen up to show himself to the world.][2]

The image of those little sunstruck windows flashing in the daylight, to which Kafka calls our special attention by insisting that there is something insane about their glint, is a more threatening transformation of the radiance. This time the passage leaves the reader with conflicted feelings, fully in the tradition of the sublime, inspiring both awe and terror.

The bizarre and striking imagery that continues the passage underscores the feeling of some fearful taboo that is near to being transgressed by K.'s gaze. In any event the passage discloses to the reader that the literal horizon of the understanding is outstripped by the metaphoric vision. The tiny windows, apertures through which some knowledge of the other side may pass, catch the light of the sun. The flashing prevents K. from seeing through them, presumably, but also signals that something violent, uncanny, possibly demonic is afoot. The image of the repressed giant bursting through the roof gives body to affect. In bursting forth through the rooftops into the deep vault of blue sky, Kafka's image enacts the power of the sublime moment to

---

[2] The Willa and Edwin Muir translation of this passage mutes the weird ambiguity that is expressed in Kafka's German, which I have tried to render in my version. The Muirs' ivy "graciously mantles" the tower, whereas Kafka's point is that something has mercifully been hidden from view. There are other such inadequacies in the Muir translation, in the same passage and throughout the novel. It is unfortunate that no new translation of *Das Schloß* has appeared in English. The critical edition of the manuscript has been in print in German since 1982. See *The Castle*, trans. Willa and Edwin Muir (New York: Knopf, 1992), 10.

crash through the material obstacle into a kind of liberation that is not otherwise accessible to representation.

The ambiguous force that the giant represents is indestructible and irrepressible, a permanent feature of human nature that is simultaneously in K. and in every other individual in the village. The Kafkan sublime is within and beyond the individual, both at the same time. It rises up in both K. and Frieda when they lose themselves in the spontaneity of erotic bliss on the tavern floor. When I cited this passage in the section on the feminist reception of *Das Schloß*, it revealed Kafka to be a man of his era, at least with respect to the construction of feminine sexuality. The fuller view of sexuality, however, is linked to the experience of the sublime as being suddenly freed of time and space. Frieda lies next to K., as if rendered powerless by love, in a state of ecstasy and K. too gives himself over to the voluptuous pleasure that is, emphatically, shared with Frieda:

> Dort vergiengen Stunden, Stunden gemeinsamen Atems, gemeinsamen Herzschlags, Stunden, in denen K. immerfort das Gefühl hatte, er verirre sich oder er sei soweit in der Fremde, wie vor ihm noch kein Mensch, eine Fremde, in der selbst die Luft keinen Bestandteil der Heimatluft habe, in der man vor Fremdheit ersticken müsse und in deren unsinnigen Verlockungen man doch nichts tun könne als weiter gehn, weiter sich verirren. (S 68–69)

> [Hours passed there, hours of shared breath, shared heartbeat, hours in which K. continuously had the feeling he was losing himself or had strayed farther into foreign parts than anyone before him, into a foreign world in which even the air was nothing like the air at home, in which one might suffocate on the foreignness and within whose mad enticements one could do nothing but continue on, continue to lose oneself.]

As it happens, one of the Zürau aphorisms conceptually glosses the relation of erotic pleasure to spirituality. "Die sinnliche Liebe täuscht über die himmlische hinweg; allein könnte sie es nicht, aber da sie das Element der himmlischen Liebe unbewußt in sich hat, kann sie es" (NS2:130, §79): Sensual love deceives us of heavenly love; but it could not do so alone. Because it unknowingly contains heavenly love within it, the deception is possible. Erotic experience is one of the moments in which a rift opens up in the material world, a sudden and sublime dislocation in the merely material that introduces K. into a more rarified atmosphere of human being. The superiority of the fictional passage over the aphoristic one should be plain. The metaphorics of the novel are more gripping, more truly in the spirit of Kafka's powerful imagination than the conventional, imaginatively weak metaphors of heavenly and sensual love.

When the sublime releases him from its grip, K. regains his calculating self-possession. Passionate experience cannot last, of course, but the problem is not that it does not last but that it fails to leave its mark on his imagination or moral life. K. resists the experience entirely, refusing to allow it to affect his conscious thought and deeds. He thinks not of Frieda but only that his "lapse" must have harmed his plans to master the castle. So he retreats into the rational, instrumental self and begins to treat Frieda as if he possessed her as he might possess a tool. She is now a pawn in what he thinks is his duel with Klamm.

But Klamm is K.'s double: uncanny, grotesque, and comic all at the same time. He represents the reified, alienated image of K.'s own sorry spirit. That is why K. shares the initial "K" with him, makes love to his woman, sits in his coach, drinks his cognac, and thinks about him all the time. He is to Klamm as Jekyll is to Hyde. But Klamm is also everyone's double. And if Klamm always looks different, depending on time and place and who the observer is, it is because the inner life is temporal, unfixed, permanently unreconciled.

From the perspective of the sublime, then, K. is mistaken about everything. Contrary to his fears, the surrender to human spontaneity was not a moment of contemptible weakness but a true victory over Klamm, both for him and for Frieda. They defy his deadening authority. The stayed bureaucrat embodies the anti-instinctive impulse toward planning, ordering, and rational exploitation. For K. it is as if Frieda were a natural resource. But the ecology here, as K. does not realize, is spiritual, not material. However briefly, Frieda liberated something in K. that needed to be set free. The lordly gentleman Klamm personifies a bureaucratization of the soul. He is the antithesis of spontaneity and submission of self to other. K.'s postcoital recovery of his usual scheming self, the self that exploits Frieda's honest affection for him, signals Klamm's victory over K., the strangulation of love freely offered and given (air and breathing are metaphors linked to life itself). Still, the experience has opened up a sudden crack in the unbroken surface of K.'s prosaic reality, giving him a perspective on his own soul that he, though not the reader, chooses to reject.[3]

---

[3] K.'s refusal to see and accept what is most obvious is a trait shared with his predecessor Josef K. The trick of reading both novels involves grasping what the protagonist fails to grasp, understanding what Kafka is showing rather than what he is saying. In

There are other such moments in which the sublime tears a hole in the empirical to intimate what lies beyond. One occurs near the end of the first chapter, during K.'s failed attempt to ride up to the castle in Gerstäcker's little pony-drawn sled:

> Das Schloß dort oben, merkwürdig dunkel schon, das K. heute noch zu erreichen gehofft hatte, entfernte sich wieder. Als sollte ihm noch zu vorläufigem Abschied ein Zeichen gegeben werden, erklang dort ein Glockenton, fröhlich beschwingt, eine Glocke, die wenigstens einen Augenblick lang das Herz erbeben ließ, so als drohe ihm — denn auch schmerzlich war der Klang — die Erfüllung dessen, wonach er sich unsicher sehnte. (S 29)

> [The castle above, which was already strangely dark and which K. had hoped to reach today, withdrew again. As if a sign of temporary leave-taking were being given to him, a bell pealed, merry and bright, a bell that at least for a moment made his heart tremble as if he were being threatened — for the sound was also painful — with the fulfillment of that for which he uncertainly longed.]

What "fulfillment" can this be? The "vague longing" strongly recalls Bergel-Gronemann's explanation of Jewish messianism. The object of longing must remain unnamed because it obeys the prohibition against images of the messianic, what Kafka would more likely call the pure, the true, the indestructible.

The bell passage offers a fine and characteristic example of the operation of Kafkan sublimity. The protagonist is suddenly taken by surprise, momentarily torn out of his prosaic world. Terror, pain, merriment, and longing intermingle, temporally encapsulated in an epiphanic experience. And the narrator tactfully declines to name the hidden and forbidden object of desire ("unsicher" because its object is an unstable kenesis beyond fixed naming or unmediated apprehension). The sound of the bell does not define the unnamed but merely

---

passing, we should also note that the sublime undergirds *Der Proceß* as well. Kafka's touch with it is ironic in a comic sense, beginning with the failure of his breakfast to appear in the novel's second line. As the text puts it (with sublime understatement): "Die Köchin der Frau Grubach, seiner Zimmervermieterin, die ihm jeden Tag gegen acht Uhr früh das Frühstück brachte, kam diesmal nicht. Das war noch niemals geschehn." It is the first shocking rift of many to open up in Josef K.'s thoroughly and inhumanly bureaucratized existence. Kafka's observance of the Bilderverbot in *Der Proceß* is as rigorous as in *Das Schloß*. Josef K.'s trial is best understood as a man's reluctant confrontation with his own conscience; and the conscience, spiritual site of the knowledge of good and evil, transcends representation (Dowden 1986).

points to its unsuspected proximity. The experience does not last. The sublime call gives way to an ordinary tinkling of ordinary bells.

Immediately after the bell scene, K. meets the uncanny twins, his "helpers" Artur and Jeremias. Significantly, the otherwise mirthless K. laughs when he first sees them. Jeremias later points out to K. that it was their assignment to cheer him up; Galater dispatched them expressly for that purpose (S 367). The assistants, funny and creepy at the same time, are the living return of the repressed, and K. treats them accordingly. He beats them cruelly, ultimately driving them away.

The twins doubly embody K.'s repressed capacity for mirth, play, and sensual pleasure. That is why they are present during K.'s lovemaking with Frieda and not, as Kundera supposes, because K. is under surveillance by the state. In this capacity they too are signs of Kafka's anthropological absolute, odd creatures who come from the castle but belong also to K. The absolute is individual and common to all, simultaneously within and without, immanent and transcendent.

My final example of the Kafkan sublime combines elements of all the others: light, the body, silence. When K. goes to visit Olga, he meets Amalia and has a conversation with her. The frosty Amalia is less than forthcoming, but it turns out that speech is not her most revealing mode:

> Amalia lächelte und dieses Lächeln, trotzdem es traurig war, erhellte das düster zusammengezogene Gesicht, machte die Stummheit sprechend, machte die Fremdheit vertraut, war die Preisgabe eines Geheimnisses, die Preisgabe eines bisher behüteten Besitzes, der zwar wieder zurückgenommen werden konnte, aber niemals mehr ganz. (S 265)

> [Amalia smiled and this smile, even though it was sad, illuminated her grimly drawn face, made her silence speak, made the foreignness familiar, was the giving away of a secret, the giving away of a possession that up to now had been carefully guarded and could be taken back again, but could never again be taken back completely.]

This passage gives the scale of the Kafkan sublime. It has nothing of the cataclysmic, monumental scale associated with Romanticism and its preoccupation with natural disaster and revolution. Kafkan sublimity has to do with human identity, a bond that is individual and common. Amalia's smile breaks through the hard shell of ice that surrounds her, and it gives off a light that clarifies her face and establishes a humane contact with K. that exceeds words. It does not last. She retracts the smile, to be sure, but the narrator is at pains to point out that once made, the contact cannot be broken entirely. As with the ivy-covered castle tower, some secret has been betrayed, and something hidden has now seen the light of day.

Amalia's smile requires no elaborate exegesis. Its human meaning is straightforward. The light of her smile is the sublime of human intimacy. What requires explanation is its place in the larger setting of the novel. It reiterates Kafka's non-mimetic strategy of intimating rather that describing the object of his narrative effort. That object is the transcendent, spiritual realm that lies beyond words and individuality. But it is not the divine, completely other realm of religion. It is the human contact that Kafka had so much trouble establishing during his lifetime, but that he was keenly aware of. It has a utopian, even messianic dimension that dictates Kafka's elaborately metaphorical indirection in dealing with it in the language of fiction.

Kafka's fiction as a whole and the aphorisms in particular demonstrate unmistakably that the transcendent remains permanently out of reach. The exception to this rule, as I have been arguing, are the few rifts opened up by the scattering of sublime moments throughout the text. They do not offer themselves as a highroad to transcendence but serve only as an assurance that something is there in the nontime and nonspace of the human soul, something worth aspiring to even if it remains out of reach. K.'s unnamed ambition, his motive for wanting to penetrate the castle, is utopian. There is no method and no theory and no eschatology associated with it. Its literary corollary is meaning, which remains always present, always ahead, and always other.

K. aims for the good life but goes about achieving it in ways that make it even more distant. His exploitation of Frieda and his abuse of his assistants, which he supposes will further his interests, only alienate him more deeply from what he most ardently desires. He is like one of the crows from a Kafka aphorism who want to smash the heavens.

> Die Krähen behaupten, eine einzige Krähe könnte den Himmel zerstören. Das ist zweifellos, beweist aber nichts gegen den Himmel, denn Himmel bedeutet eben: Unmöglichkeit von Krähen.

> [The crows claim that a single crow can destroy the heavens. That is beyond doubt, but it proves nothing against heaven, for heaven simply means: impossibility of crows.]

Utopia means the impossibility of K. His repressed, self-absorbed, abusive nature *is* the castle that prevents him from achieving his own aim. But seen rightly, Kafka's pessimism is not so dark as it has traditionally been perceived. It has an uncompromising moral edge that has seldom come into view.

Ethics and Irony

What are the cultural politics of Kafkan sublimity? Is Kafka's anthropology the sign of a political culpability, a failure of liberal, democratic instincts? I do not think that Kafka's literary exploration of the soul compromises him ethically any more than Robert Musil's similar explorations do him (in *Vereinigungen* and the latter parts of *Der Mann ohne Eigenschaften*), or than William James's scientific exploration of mysticism compromises James.

Kafka does not offer his anthropological absolute as an article of political commitment, and it is not likely to be applied as one, not even in the clamorous political subculture of contemporary literary theory and criticism. Harold Bloom may be right when he claims that Kafka has had a lasting impact on the shape of modern Judaism, or at least among intellectuals, but such influence is not charged with a politically measurable, ideological valence. This is true at least partly because Western political culture remains currently stable. It was otherwise in Kafka's time.

In the Weimar era, mysticism and reaction were closely allied, especially in Germany. Ernst Jünger's thought, also an anthropology of sorts, carries with it a heroic, more or less Nietzschean ethic with plainly political implications. Kafka's does not. Nor does Kafka in any way suggest or imply that mysticism is a more profound alternative to public thought and action than politics. He is distant from the quasi-religious cult of art associated with Stefan George and his acolytes, and he is distant from the apolitical aesthetic snobbery of the early Thomas Mann. But he is also distant from Brecht's exaggerated insistence on a direct, didactic link between art and politics. Kafka's fiction is the vehicle of autonomously imaginative exploration. As Adorno has shown, Kafka is not easily co-opted by any ideological agenda, which would include, we might add, even the cultural Zionism that was closest to his indecisive heart.

Moreover, Kafka did not claim for himself or his writing a revolutionary social role. Art's place in politics is modest, which means that Lionel Trilling was right when he fretted that Kafka was probably indifferent to the kind of liberalism that undergirds the cultures in which his books are read, admired, and discussed. It was not the world in which he lived. In addition, he never said anything about creating a new kind of human being or a new kind of society. He was interested in exploring the spiritual depths of the versions that he knew, trying to understand them better. There is no point in his fiction at which his mystical anthropology threatens to reverse dialectically into a political expression. His fiction points neither toward activism of commitment nor toward the quietism that passively awaits the coming of the Messiah. Our activities in public life are likely to remain unaffected by Kafka, even though his influence on our collective imagination has been substantial.

If anything, Kafka's cultural politics resemble Freud's. Just as Lionel Trilling feared, neither of them shared our confidence in the liberalism upon which Western democracies are based. They were living and writing at a time and in a place in which liberal culture, the cornerstone of Jewish emancipation in the Habsburg lands, lay in ruins. Kafka's turn to a mystical anthropology probably shares its deepest motive with Freud's turn to psychoanalysis. The latter's *Interpretation of Dreams* (1900) carries with it an epigraph that applies to Kafka as well: "If I cannot shake the higher powers, I will stir up the depths." Together, Freud and Kafka have turned out to be our century's preeminent stirrers of the depths.

The retreat from politics in favor of art and psychology was, as Carl Schorske has shown (1980), characteristic for the dissolution of the Habsburg era. Kafka's unwillingness to put his faith in a new politics (or an old religion) is no more remarkable than Freud's parallel impulses. Both of them shunned the treacheries, uncertainties, and compromises of political engagement for what, from their perspective at least, seemed realms of spirit that were ahistorical, noncontingent. Even if they could not transform the status quo, they at least converted their generation's experience into powerful myths, visions of the world that, if not exactly reassuring, could be lived with: one poetic, the other scientific (more or less), both great narrative achievements.

Both Kafka and Freud were pessimists. They did not expect much in the way of improvement, least of all in human nature. But the myths they offered were and remain a consolation simply by transforming shared experience into objective aesthetic form. In thus transforming shared experience they lift it into a realm that makes it manageable by making it discussable, putting it on a human scale. If Gregor Samsa in particular has achieved the status of cultural icon — and still does not need the artificial life-support system of university teaching to survive in the public imagination — it must be because practically everyone can at some time identify with his experience. One gets the irrepressible feeling that Kafka has somehow hit the nail right on the head.

But what about the cultural politics of *Das Schloß* now, in a post-Cold War age that is politically stable yet extraordinarily conscious of ideological tensions within the overarching consensus? The features that define the moral identity of *Das Schloß* and Kafka in general when interrogated from the perspective of his sociopolitical meaning are the novel's irony and skeptical detachment from both culture and politics. Perhaps the irony is clearest in *Josefine, die Sängerin*, a communitarian reverie in which the artist's gift and social role are respected but in which her claim to exemption from average mouse responsibilities (for example, political responsibility) are treated with skepticism. Politically the mouse-folk is on its own, without direction from a charismatic figure. Each mouse must contribute. The artist is not its Führerin and is not exempt from responsibility.

As I noted earlier, there is no spiritual leader in *Das Schloß*, no priest, pastor, or rabbi. Another stock figure conspicuous in its absence from the novel is the artist. There is no figure in the village comparable to Titorelli of *Der Proceß*. But even if there were (and some critics take the secretary Momus as a diminished writer of sorts), it would make no difference. Art too tends to obey the law of reification. Titorelli's pictures are all the same: simple, dreary, lifeless landscapes. As Titorelli points out to Josef K., everything belongs to the court; there can be no escape from its law, least of all in what passes for art within its sphere of influence.

Likewise, in K.'s world everybody and everything must obey the law of the castle. Momus simply records what he hears. No imagination is involved. The castle's "law" is its all-consuming bureaucratic order, a deadening calcification of the human spirit. Reification, doctrine, dogma, conformism — all name the law that ideology obeys. It is worth remembering that Kafka was deeply alienated by the biblical Abraham, whose dogmatic faith was such that he was ready to kill his son for God the way a waiter might fill a customer's order. Kafka may not have had a politics, but his ethical sensibilities, his response to doctrine and dogmatic authority, is compatible with liberal habits of mind. With a supremely deadpan gaze, Kafka satirizes conformism in *Das Schloß*, which is to say that he distances himself and his reader from it by depicting it at its worst. To take that image as Kafka's view of reality too seriously, or seriously in the wrong way, as if it were social realism without the piercing comic irony that gives it its penetrating insight, underestimates the power and nature of his imagination. He offers *Das Schloß* as an ironic perspective on the world, not as its mimetic likeness.

In contemporary political life — that is, in the transactions that occur daily in our Western, middle-class, liberal culture — the "message"
of *Das Schloß*, if it can be said to have anything as crude as a message at
all, might sound something like this: the good life remains at all times
both within us and ahead of us; it cannot be hurried or forced into
submission but must be courted gradually, and above all with attention
to the anthropological absolute that, when allowed to break through
the bureaucratic encrustation that bears down on the human spirit like
snow on cottage roofs, will join us wholesomely to others.

Admittedly, to extract a flat-footed moral like this from a Kafka
novel is grotesquely reductive, both diminishing the text and implicitly
attempting to co-opt the experience of the prospective reader by
steering her or his response. But neither is the simplification completely wrong-headed. It is in error simply because it names what is incommensurable with language and therefore falsifies everything that
Kafka intimated, with infinite tact and imaginative resource, without
ever resorting to fixed concepts and static names.

Works Consulted

Kant, Immanuel (1790). *Critique of Judgment.* Trans. Werner S. Pluhar. Indianapolis: Hackett, 1987.

Graetz, Heinrich (1897). *Geschichte der Juden von den ältesten Zeiten bis auf die Gegenwart.* 11 vols. Leipzig: O. Leiner, 1897–1911.

Fromer, Jakob (1909). *Der Organismus des Judentums.* Charlottenburg: Selbstverlag des Verfassers.

Pinès, Meyer Isser (1911). *Histoire de la littérature judéo-allemande.* Paris: Jouve.

Bergel-Gronemann, Elfride (1921). "Der Messiasgedanke." *Der Jude* 6:268–627.

Brod, Max (1926). "Nachwort zu Franz Kafkas Roman *Das Schloß.*"

Hašek, Jaroslav (1926). *Die Abenteuer des braven Soldaten Schwejk.* Trans. Grete Reiner. Prague: Synek.

Kracauer, Siegfried (1926). "*Das Schloß*: Zu Franz Kafkas Nachlaßroman." *Frankfurter Zeitung*, 28 November, morning edition. Reprinted in Born, 1983:139–42.

Kafka, Franz (1930). *The Castle.* Trans. Edwin Muir and Willa Muir. New York: Knopf.

Broch, Hermann (1936). "James Joyce und die Gegenwart." *Schriften zur Literatur 1.* Ed. Paul Michael Lützeler. Frankfurt am Main: Suhrkamp, 1975, 63–95.

Hurston, Zora Neale (1937). *Their Eyes Were Watching God.* New York: Lippincott.

Camus, Albert (1942). "L'Espoir et l'absurde dans l'oeuvre de Franz Kafka." *Le Mythe de Sisyphe.* Paris: Gallimard. Trans. in Flores 1946:251–61 and Gray 1962:147–156.

Arendt, Hannah. 1944a. "Franz Kafka: A Revaluation." *Partisan Review* 11:412–22. Reprinted in *Essays in Understanding 1930–1954.* Ed. Jerome Kohn. New York: Harcourt Brace, 1994, 69–80.

Arendt, Hannah. 1944b. "The Jew as Pariah. A Hidden Tradition." *Jewish Social Studies* 6:99–122; in German: *Sechs Essays*. Heidelberg: Schneider, 1948. Reprinted in English in *The Jew as Pariah: Jewish Identity and Politics in the Modern Age*. Ed. Ron Feldman. New York: Grove Press, 1978, 67–90.

Flores, Angel, ed. (1946). *The Kafka Problem*. New York: New Directions.

Anders, Günther (1947). "Franz Kafka — pro und contra." *Die Neue Rundschau* 58:119–57.

Goodman, Paul (1947). *Kafka's Prayer*. New York: Vanguard.

Ong, Walter J. (1947). "Kafka's Castle in the West." *Thought* 22:439–60.

Politzer, Heinz (1947). "Von Mendelssohn zu Franz Kafka. The Jewish Man of Letters in Germany." *Commentary* 6:344–351.

Sartre, Jean-Paul (1947). "Animadab ou le fantastique considéré comme un langage." *Situations I*. Paris. "Aminadab or the Fantastic Considered as Language." *Literary and Philosophical Essays*. Trans. Anette Michelson. New York: Macmillan, 1965.

Tauber, Herbert (1948). *Franz Kafka: An Interpretation of His Works*. New Haven: Yale University Press.

Blanchot, Maurice (1949). "Le langage de la fiction." *La part du feu*. Paris: Gallimard.

Goldschmidt, Hermann Levin (1949). "The Key to Kafka. What is his True Significance?" *Commentary* 8:129–38.

Broch, Hermann (1950). "Hugo von Hofmannsthals Prosaschriften." *Schriften zur Literatur und Kritik 1*. Ed. Paul Michael Lützeler. Kommentierte Werkausgabe, vol. 9/1. Frankfurt am Main: Suhrkamp, 285–336.

Lewis, R. W. B. (1950). "Lionel Trilling and the New Stoicism." *Hudson Review* 3:313–17.

Trilling, Lionel (1950). *The Liberal Imagination: Essays on Literature and Society*. London: Mercury Books, 1961.

Anders, Günther (1951). *Franz Kafka: Pro und Contra*. Munich: Beck.

Janouch, Gustav (1951). *Gespräche mit Kafka*. Frankfurt am Main: Fischer.

Jens, Walter (1951). "Kafka: Eine vorläufige Analyse seiner Welt und seines Werkes." *Deutsche Universitätszeitung* 6.1:13–17.

Seidel, Bruno (1951). "Franz Kafkas Vision des Totalitarismus. Politische Gedanken zu Kafkas Roman *Das Schloß* und Orwells Utopie *1984*." *Die Besinnung* 6:11–14.

Webster, Peter Dow (1951). "A Critical Examination of Franz Kafka's *The Castle*." *American Imago* 8:3–28.

Heller, Erich (1952). "The World of Franz Kafka." *The Disinherited Mind*. Cambridge: Bowes and Bowes.

Walser, Martin (1952). *Beschreibung einer Form. Versuch über Franz Kafka*. 2d ed. Munich: Hanser, 1963.

Adorno, Theodor (1953). "Aufzeichnungen zu Kafka," *Die Neue Rundschau* 64:325–53.

Auerbach, Erich (1953). *Mimesis: The Representation of Reality in Western Literature*. Trans. Willard Trask. Princeton: Princeton University Press.

Emrich, Wilhelm (1954). "Zur Ästhetik der modernen Dichtung." *Akzente* 1:371–87.

Mann, Thomas (1954). "Homage." Franz Kafka, *The Castle*. New York: Random House.

Martini, Fritz (1954). "Franz Kafka *Das Schloß*." *Das Wagnis der Sprache*. Stuttgart: Klett.

Emrich, Wilhelm (1956). "Die Literaturrevolution und die moderne Gesellschaft." *Akzente* 3:173–191; translated in Emrich 1971.

Gray, Ronald (1956). *Kafka's Castle*. Cambridge: At the University Press.

Jens, Walter (1957). *Statt einer Literaturgeschichte*. Pfullingen: Neske.

Adorno, Theodor (1958). "Erpreßte Versöhnung." *Der Monat* 11, No. 122: 37–49; *Gesammelte Schriften*. Frankfurt am Main: Suhrkamp, 1974, 11/2: 251–80.

Emrich, Wilhelm (1958a). *Franz Kafka*. Bonn: Athenäum; *Franz Kafka: A Critical Study of His Writings*. Trans. S. Z. Buehne. New York: Ungar, 1984.

Emrich, Wilhelm (1958b). *Die Weltkritik von Franz Kafka*. Mainz: Akademie für Wissenschaft und Literatur.

Flores, Angel, and Homer Swander, eds. (1958). *Franz Kafka Today*. Madison: University of Wisconsin Press.

Lukács, Georg (1958). *Wider den mißverstandenen Realismus*. Hamburg: Claasen. *The Meaning of Contemporary Realism*. Trans. John and Necke Mander. London: Merlin, 1962; *Realism in Our Time*. New York: Barnes and Noble.

Werfel, Franz (1959). *Die Dramen*. Vol. 1. Ed. Adolf Klarmann. Frankfurt am Main: S. Fischer.

Robert, Marthe (1960). *Kafka*. Paris: Gallimard.

Brinkmann, Richard (1961). "Hofmannsthal und die Sprache." *Deutsche Vierteljahrsschrift für Geistesgeschichte und Literaturwissenschaft* 35.1:69–95.

Robert, Marthe (1961). "Kafka en France." *Mercure de France,* 342:241–251; "Kafka in Frankreich." *Akzente* 13 (1966): 310–20.

Gray, Ronald, ed. (1962). *Kafka: A Collection of Critical Essays.* Englewood Cliffs: Prentice Hall.

Jens, Walter (1962). *Statt einer Literaturgeschichte.* 5th, expanded ed. Pfullingen: Neske.

Mayer, Hans (1962). "Kafka und kein Ende?" *Ansichten: Zur Literatur der Zeit.* Reinbek: Rowohlt, 54–70.

Politzer, Heinz (1962). *Franz Kafka: Parable and Paradox.* Ithaca: Cornell University Press. Exp. German edition *Franz Kafka der Künstler.* Frankfurt am Main: S. Fischer, 1965.

Sartre, Jean-Paul (1962). "La démilitarisation de la culture." *Situations VII.* Paris: Gallimard, 322–31; "Die Abrüstung der Kultur. Rede auf dem Weltfriedenskongreß in Moskau." *Sinn und Form* 14:805–15.

Welles, Orson (1962). *The Trial.* FRG, France, Italy: Hisa, Paris.

Emrich, Wilhelm (1963a). "Dichterischer und politischer Mythos: Ihre wechselseitige Beziehung." *Akzente* 10:191–210.

Emrich, Wilhelm (1963b). "Franz Kafka zwischen Ost und West." *Geist und Widergeist. Wahrheit und Lüge in der Literatur.* Frankfurt am Main: Athenäum, 1965, 300–310. Translated as "Franz Kafka East and West," Emrich 1971:63–78.

Goldstücker, Eduard, ed. (1963). *Franz Kafka aus Prager Sicht 1963.* Prague: Tschechoslowakische Akademie der Wissenschaften, 1965.

Kundera, Milan (1963). *The Joke.* Trans. Michael Henry Heim. New York: Harper and Row, 1982.

Robert, Marthe (1963). *L'Ancien et le Nouveau de Don Quichotte à Franz Kafka.* Paris: Payot, 1966; Trans. Carol Cosman. *The Old and the New: From Don Quixote to Kafka.* Berkeley: Univeristy of California Press, 1977.

Blanchot, Maurice (1964). "Le pont de bois." *La Nouvelle Revue Française* 12:90–103. "Die Holzbrücke." Blanchot 1993:141–52.

Kudszus, Winfried (1964). "Erzählhaltung und Zeitverschiebung in Kafkas *Prozeß* und *Schloß.*" *Deutsche Vierteljahrsschrift für Geistesgeschichte und Literaturwissenschaft* 38.2:192–207.

Mayer, Hans (1964). "Literatur und Kommunismus." *Der Monat* 16.185:49–56.

Mayer, Hans, and François Bondy (1964). "The Struggle for Kafka and Joyce." *Encounter* 22.128:83–89.

Sokel, Walter H. (1964). *Franz Kafka — Tragik und Ironie. Zur Struktur seiner Kunst.* Munich and Vienna: Langen and Müller.

Trilling, Lionel (1965). *Beyond Culture.* Oxford: Oxford University Press, 1980.

Emrich, Wilhelm (1965). "Franz Kafka Ost und West." *Geist und Widergeist: Wahrheit und Lüge in der Literatur.* Frankfurt am Main: Athenäum; Franz Kafka East and West," in Emrich 1971:63–78.

Reed, T. J. (1965). "Kafka und Schopenhauer: Philosophisches Denken und dichterisches Bild." *Euphorion* 59:160–72.

Sartre, Jean-Paul, Ernst Fischer, Eduard Goldstücker, Milan Kundera (1965). "Symposium on the Question of Decadence." Baxandall 1972:225–239.

Barthes, Roland (1966). "Le reponse de Kafka." *Essais critiques.* Paris: Editions du Seuil. "Kafka's Answer." *Critical Essays.* Trans. Richard Howard. Evanston, Illinois: Northwestern University Press.

Binder, Hartmut (1966). *Motiv und Gestaltung bei Franz Kafka.* Abhandlungen zu Kunst-, Musik-, und Literaturwissenschaft, 37. Bonn: Bouvier.

Fischer, Ernst (1966). "Der Kampf um Kafka." *Kunst und Konvention. Beitrag zu einer marxistischen Ästhetik.* Reinbek: Rowohlt, 71–74.

Philippi, Klaus-Peter (1966). *Reflexion und Wirklichkeit. Untersuchungen zu Kafkas Roman 'Das Schloß.'* Tübingen: Niemeyer.

Sokel, Walter H. (1966). *Franz Kafka.* Columbia Essays on Modern Writers, 19. New York: Columbia University Press.

Henel, Ingeborg C. (1967). "Die Deutbarkeit von Kafkas Werken." *Franz Kafka.* Ed. Heinz Politzer. Wege der Forschung, 322. Darmstadt: Wissenschaftliche Buchgesellschaft, 1973, 406–30.

Emrich, Wolfgang (1968). *Polemik: Streitschriften, Pressefehden und kritische Essays um Prinzipien, Methoden, und Maßstäbe der Literatur.* Frankfurt am Main: Athenäum.

Gysi, Klaus (1968). "Festrede anläßlich des 20. Jahrestages der Wiedereröffnung des Deutschen Nationaltheaters Weimar." *Theater der Zeit* 17:1–7, suppl.

Noelte, Rudolf (1968). *Das Schloß.* FRG: Noelte, Alfa.

Alter, Robert (1969). "On Walter Benjamin." *Commentary* 48.3:86–93.

Brod, Max (1969). *Streitbares Leben 1884–1968.* Munich: F. A. Herbig.

Burke, Kenneth (1969). "The Caricature of Courtship: Kafka." *A Rhetoric of Motives*. Berkeley: University of California Press. Reprinted in Bloom 1988a:23–33.

Neumeyer, Peter, ed. (1969). *Twentieth-Century Interpretations of "The Castle."* Englewood Cliffs: Prentice Hall.

Adorno, Theodor (1970). *Ästhetische Theorie*. Eds. Gretel Adorno and Rolf Tiedemann. Frankfurt am Main: Suhrkamp.

Anders, Günther (1970). "Reflections on My Book, *Franz Kafka Pro and Contra*." *Mosaic* 3.4:59–72.

Bahr, Erhard (1970). "Kafka and the Prague Spring." *Mosaic* 3.4:15–29.

Corngold, Stanley (1970). "Kafka's *Die Verwandlung*: Metamorphosis of Metaphor." Mosaic 3.4:91–106.

Beck, Evelyn Torton (1971). *Kafka and the Yiddish Theater: Its Impact on His Work*. Madison: University of Wisconsin Press.

Klíma, Ivan (1971). *Theaterstücke*. Lucerne: J. Bücher.

Emrich, Wilhelm (1971). *The Literary Revolution and Modern Society and Other Essays*. Trans. Alexander and Elizabeth Henderson. New York: Ungar.

Jens, Walter (1972). *Antiquierte Antike? Perspektiven eines neuen Humanismus*. Ed. Manfred von Wedemeyer. Sylter Beiträge, 1. Hamburg: Hansen and Hansen.

Beißner, Friedrich (1972). *Kafkas Darstellung des "traumhaften inneren Lebens."* Bebenhausen: L. Rotsch.

Baxandall, Lee, ed. (1972). *Radical Perspectives in the Arts*. Harmondsworth: Penguin.

Holthusen, Hans Egon (1972). "Literatur und Rechtfertigung." *Ensemble* 3:233–58.

Neesen, Peter (1972). *Franz Kafka und der Louvre-Zirkel*. Göppingen: Kümmerle.

Sebald, W. G. (1972). "The Undiscover'd Country: The Death Motif in Kafka's *Castle*." *Journal of European Studies* 2.1. Reprinted in Bloom 1988a:35–50.

Winkelmann, John (1972). "An Interpretation of Kafka's *Das Schloß*." *Monatshefte* 64:115–31.

Adorno, Theodor (1973). *Philosophische Frühschriften*. Frankfurt am Main: Suhrkamp.

Goldstücker, Eduard (1973). "Zehn Jahre nach der Kafka-Konferenz in Liblice." *Die Zeit*, No. 35 (August 24). Reprinted in Almási 1984:62–70.

Sheppard, Richard (1973). *On Kafka's Castle: A Study.* New York: Barnes and Noble.

Grimes, Margaret (1974). "Kafka's Use of Cue-Names: Its Importance for an Interpretation of *The Castle.*" *Centennial Review* 18:221–30.

Hamalian, Leo, ed. (1974). *Franz Kafka: A Collection of Criticism.* New York: McGraw-Hill.

Heller, Erich (1974). *Franz Kafka.* New York: Viking Press.

Tate, Eleanor (1974). "Kafka's The Castle: Another Dickens Novel?" *Southern Review: An Australian Journal of Literary Studies* 7:157–68.

Friedrich, Reinhard H. (1975). "K's 'bitteres Kraut' and *Exodus.*" *German Quarterly* 48:355–57.

Fülleborn, Ulrich (1975). "'Veränderung': Zu Rilkes *Malte* und Kafkas *Schloß.*" *Etudes germaniques* 30:438–54.

Goldstein, Bluma (1975). "Franz Kafka, January 1922: Therapeutic Reflections on the the Nature of Life and Literature." *Austriaca. Beiträge zur österreichischen Literatur. Festschrift für Heinz Politzer.* Eds. Winfried Kudszus, Hinrich Seeba and Richard Brinkmann. Tübingen: Niemeyer, 352–369.

Hibberd, John (1975). *Kafka in Context.* London: Studio Vista.

Kurz, Gerhard (1975). "Die Literatur, das Leben, und der Tod: Anmerkungen zu Cervantes und Kafka." *Archiv für das Studium der neueren Sprachen und Literaturen* 127:265–279.

Politzer, Heinz (1975). "The Alienated Self: A Key to Franz Kafka's Castle." *Michigan Quarterly Review* 14:398–414.

Jens, Walter (1976). *Feldzüge eines Republikaners.* Pfullingen: Neske.

Sebald, W. G. (1976). "The Law of Ignominy: Authority, Messianism, and Exile in *The Castle.*" *On Kafka: Semi-Centenary Perspectives.* Ed. Franz Kuna. London: Elek. New York: Barnes and Nobles.

Adorno, Theodor (1977). *Kulturkritik und Gesellschaft I.* Frankfurt am Main: Suhrkamp.

Bernheimer, Charles (1977). "Symbolic Bond and Textual Play: Structure of *The Castle.*" Flores 1977:367–84.

Flores, Angel, ed. (1977). *The Kafka Debate.* New York: Gordian.

Kurz, Gerhard (1977). "Eine autobiographische Deutung Kafkas: Binders altneue Sicht auf den Roman *Das Schloß.*" *Neue Rundschau* 88:113–20.

Roth, Philip (1977). *The Professor of Desire.* New York: Farrar Straus Giroux.

Pott, Hans-Georg (1977). "Das Schloß." *Kürbiskern* 2:83–95.

Arneson, Richard. (1978). "Power and Authority in *The Castle.*" *Mosaic* 12:99–113. Reprinted in Bloom 1988a:107–24.

Caputo-Mayr, Marie Luise, ed. (1978). *Franz Kafka: Eine Aufsatzsammlung nach einem Symposium in Philadelphia.* Berlin: Agora.

Emrich, Wilhelm (1978). "Franz Kafka und der literarische Nihilismus." In Caputo-Mayr 1978:108–25.

Kazin, Alfred (1978). *New York Jew.* London: Secker and Warburg.

Kudszus, Winfried (1978). "Musik im *Schloß* und in *Josefine die Sängerin.*" *Modern Austrian Literature* 11:248–256.

Sokel, Walther H. (1978). "Kafka's Poetics of the Inner Self." *Modern Austrian Literature* 11:37–58.

Binder, Hartmut, ed. (1979). *Kafka-Handbuch in zwei Bänden.* Vol. 2. *Das Werk und seine Wirkung.* Stuttgart: Kröner.

Bovenschen, Sylvia (1979). *Die imaginierte Weiblichkeit. Exemplarische Untersuchungen zur kulturgeschichtlichen und literarischen Präsentationsformen des Weiblichen.* Frankfurt am Main: Suhrkamp.

Krusche, Dietrich (1979). "Kafka als Schulklassiker." Binder 1979:860–71.

Kundera, Milan (1979). "Quelque part là-derrière." *L'Art du roman.* Paris: Gallimard, 1986, 123–46. "Somewhere Behind." *The Art of the Novel.* Trans. Linda Asher. New York: Grove Press, 1987, 99–120.

Robert, Marthe (1979). *Seul, comme Franz Kafka.* Paris: Calmann-Lévy. *As Lonely as Franz Kafka.* Trans. Ralph Manheim. New York: Harcourt Brace Jovanovich, 1982.

Sokel, Walter H. (1979). "Language and Truth in the Two Worlds of Franz Kafka." *German Quarterly* 52:364–384.

Sheppard, Richard (1979). "*Das Schloß*". In Binder 1979:441–70.

Sussman, Henry (1979). "The Circle of Exclusion: A Reading of *The Castle*," *Franz Kafka: Geometrician of Metaphor.* Madison: Coda Press, 113–146.

Finkielkraut, Alain (1980). *Le Juif imaginaire.* Paris: Editions du Seuil; *The Imaginary Jew.* Trans. Kevin O'Neill and David Suchoff. Lincoln: University of Nebraska, 1994.

Fülleborn, Ulrich (1980). "Der Einzelne und die 'geistige Welt': Zu Kafkas Romanen." *Franz Kafka: Themen und Probleme.* Ed. Claude David. Göttingen: Vandenhoek and Ruprecht.

Henel, Ingeborg C. (1980). "Kafka als Denker." *Franz Kafka. Themen und Probleme.* Ed. Claude David. Göttingen: Vandenhoeck and Ruprecht, 48–65.

Kudszus, Winfried (1980). "Reflections on Kafka's Critique of Knowledge." *Newsletter of the Kafka Society of America.* 4:3–6.

Schorske, Carl E. (1980). *Fin-de-siècle Vienna: Politics and Culture.* New York: Knopf.

Sizemore, Christine W. (1980). "Cognitive Dissonance and the Anxiety of Response to Kafka's *The Castle.*" *Comparatist* 4:23–30.

Weeks, Andrew (1980). "Kafka's *Das Schloß.*" *Paradox of the Employee: Variants of a Social Theme in Modern Literature.* German Studies in America, vol. 35. Berne: Peter Lang, 81–119.

Benjamin, Walter (1981). *Benjamin über Kafka.* Ed. Hermann Schwepphäuser. Frankfurt am Main: Suhrkamp.

Blanchot, Maurice (1981). *De Kafka à Kafka.* Paris: Gallimard. *Von Kafka zu Kafka.* Trans. Elsbeth Dangel. Frankfurt am Main: Fischer Taschenbuch, 1993.

Emrich, Wilhelm (1981). *Freiheit und Nihilismus in der Literatur des 20. Jahrhunderts.* Akademie der Wissenschaften und der Literatur, Abhandlungen der Klasse der Literatur 1981/82, vol. 3. Wiesbaden: Steiner.

Hoffman, Anne Golumb (1981). "Plotting the Landscape: Stories and Storytellers in *The Castle.*" *Twentieth-Century Literature* 27:289–307.

Kempf, Franz R. (1981). "Das Bild des Bettes und seine Funktion in Kafkas Romanen." *Sprache und Literatur*, 89–97. Frankfurt am Main: Lang.

Bernheimer, Charles (1982). *Flaubert and Kafka: Studies in Psychopoetic Structure.* New Haven: Yale University Press.

Pascal, Roy (1982). *Kafka's Narrators: A Study of his Stories and Sketches.* Cambridge: Cambridge University Press.

Beißner, Friedrich (1983). *Der Erzähler Franz Kafka und andere Vorträge.* Frankfurt am Main: Suhrkamp.

Binder, Hartmut (1983). "Schreiben als Kur: Das Schloß." *Kafka. Der Schaffensprozeß*, 306–346. Frankfurt am Main: Suhrkamp.

Born, Jürgen, ed. (1983). *Franz Kafka: Kritik und Rezeption 1924–1938.* Edited in collaboration with Elke Koch, Herbert Mühlfeit, Mercedes Treckman. Frankfurt am Main: S. Fischer.

Goozé, Marjanne E. (1983). "Texts, Textuality, and Silence in Franz Kafka's *Castle.*" *Modern Language Notes* 98.3. Reprinted in Bloom 1988a:125–40.

Kessler, Susanne (1983). *Kafka — Poetik des sinnlichen Lebens. Strukturen sprachkritischen Erzählens.* Germanistische Abhandlungen, 53. Stuttgart: Metzler.

Koelb, Clayton (1983). "Kafka's Rhetorical Moment." *PMLA* 98:37–46.

Nutting, Peter West (1983). "Kafka's 'strahlende Heiterkeit': Discursive Humor and Comic Narrative in *Das Schloß*." *Deutsche Vierteljahrsschrift für Geistesgeschichte und Literaturwissenschaft* 57:651–78.

Almási, Miklós, et al. (1984). *Franz Kafka. Nachwirkungen eines Dichters.* Munich: Pfeiffer.

Anders, Günther (1984). *Mensch ohne Welt. Schriften zu Kunst und Literatur.* Munich: Beck.

Cooke, Michael (1984). *Afro-American Literature in the Twentieth Century: The Achievement of Intimacy.* New Haven: Yale University Press.

Goldstücker, Eduard (1984). "Zur Ost-West-Auseinandersetzung über Franz Kafka." Almási et al. 1984:47–61.

Hoffer, Klaus (1984). "In der Strafkolonie. Bemerkungen zu Kafkas *Schloß.*" *Manuskripte* 24:8–12.

Klein, Alan (1984). "Kafka's *The Castle*." *Explicator* 42.3:43–45.

Middel, Eike (1984). "Kafkas Romanfragment *Das Schloß.* Probleme der Interpretation und der Forschung." *Weimarer Beiträge* 30:885–89.

Shaked, Gerschom (1984). "The Kafka Syndrome." *Jerusalem Quarterly* 33:64–78.

Goetschel, Willi Hayum (1985). "Kafka's Negative Dialectics." *Journal of the Kafka Society of America* 9:83–106.

Jens, Walter (1985). "'Laßt den Menschen nicht verkommen!' Zu Franz Kafka, *Das Schloß.*" Jens and Küng 1985:306–24.

Jens, Walter, and Hans Küng (1985). *Dichtung und Religion.* Munich: Kindler.

Küng, Hans (1985). "Religion im Zusammenbruch der Moderne. Zu Franz Kafka, *Das Schloß.*" Jens and Küng 1985:286–305.

Mosse, George L. (1985). *Nationalism and Sexuality: Middle-Class Morality and Sexual Norms in Modern Europe.* Madison: University of Wisconsin Press.

Mayer, Hans (1985). "Walter Benjamin und Franz Kafka." *Aufklärung heute: Reden und Aufsätze 1978–1984.* Frankfurt am Main: Suhrkamp, 45–70.

Robertson, Ritchie (1985). *Kafka: Judaism, Politics and Literature.* Oxford: Clarendon.

Sebald, W. G. (1985). "Das Gesetz der Schande — Macht, Messianismus, und Exil in Kafkas *Schloß.*" *Manuskripte* 25:117–21.

Campbell, Karen J. (1986). "Kafka's Schloß and the Subversion of Plot." *Journal of English and Germanic Philology* 85:386–403.

Dowden, Stephen D. (1986). *Sympathy for the Abyss. A Study in the Novel of German Modernism: Kafka, Broch, Musil, and Thomas Mann.* Studien zur deutschen Literatur, 90. Tübingen: Niemeyer.

Zeller, Hans (1986). "Zur Deutbarkeit von Kafkas Roman *Das Schloß.*" *Im Dialog mit der Moderne. Jacob Steiner zum 60. Geburtstag.* Frankfurt am Main: Athenäum, 276–92.

Beck, Evelyn Torton (1987). "Kafka's Traffic in Women: Gender, Power, and Sexuality." *The Dove and the Mole: Kafka's Journey into Darkness and Creativity.* Eds. Moshe Lazar and Ronald Gottermann. Malibu: Undena, 95–107.

Bloom, Allan (1987). *The Closing of the American Mind.* New York: Simon and Schuster.

Bloom, Harold (1987). *The Strong Light of the Canonical: Kafka, Freud, and Scholem as Revisionists of Jewish Culture and Thought.* New York: The City College.

Gray, Richard (1987). *Constructive Destruction. Kafka's Aphorism: Literary Tradition and Literary Transformation.* Studien zur deutschen Literatur, 91. Tübingen: Niemeyer.

Grözinger, Karl Erich, et al., eds. (1987). *Franz Kafka und das Judentum.* Frankfurt am Main: Athenäum.

Kundera, Milan (1987). *The Art of the Novel.* Trans. Linda Asher. New York: Grove Press.

Poirier, Richard (1987). "Modernism and its Difficulties." *The Renewal of Literature: Emersonian Reflections.* New York: Random House, 95–113.

Ronell, Avital (1987). "Doing Kafka in *The Castle.*" *Kafka and the Contemporary Critical Performance: Centenary Essays.* Ed. Allan Udoff. Bloomington: Indiana University Press, 214–35.

Stach, Reiner (1987). *Kafkas erotischer Mythos. Eine ästhetische Konstruktion des Weiblichen.* Frankfurt am Main: Fischer Taschenbuch.

Straub, Martin (1987). "Lesenlernen von Peter Weiss. Gedanken zu seiner Neukrantz-Kafka Rezeption in der *Ästhetik des Widerstands.*" *Weimarer Beiträge* 33:481–488.

Wald, Alan M. (1987). *The New York Intellectuals: The Rise and Decline of the Anti-Stalinist Left from the 1930s to the 1980s.* Chapel Hill: University of North Carolina Press.

Witte, Bernd (1987). "'Hier wird viel geschrieben' — Kommentar zu einigen Passagen aus Kafkas Roman *Das Schloß.*" Grözinger 1987:238–252.

Zimmermann, Hans Dieter (1987). "klam a mam? Zu Kafkas Roman *Das Schloß.*" Grözinger 1987:224–237.

Barnouw, Dagmar (1988). *Weimar Intellectuals and the Threat of Modernity.* Bloomington: Indiana University Press.

Bloom, Harold, ed. (1988a). *Franz Kafka's "The Castle."* New York: Chelsea House.

Bloom, Harold (1988b). *Poetics of Influence.* Ed. and intro. John Hollander. New Haven: Henry R. Schwab, 347–68.

Hirsch, E. D. (1988). *Cultural Literacy: What Every American Needs to Know.* New York: Vintage Books.

Mayer, Hans (1988). "Parabeln der Unmenschlichkeit." *Die umerzogene Literatur. Deutsche Schriftsteller und Bücher 1945–1967.* Berlin: Siedler, 72–77.

Baumgart, Reinhard (1989). "'Laß die Deutungen!' sagte K." *Romane von gestern — heute gelesen.* Ed. Marcel Reich-Ranicki. Vol. 2. Frankfurt am Main: S. Fischer, 30–39.

Bloom, Harold (1989). *Ruin the Sacred Truths: Poetry and Belief from the Bible to the Present.* Cambridge: Harvard University Press.

Goldstücker, Eduard (1989). *Prozesse. Erfahrungen eines Mitteleuropäers.* Trans. Friedrich Uttitz. Munich: Knaus.

Pasley, Malcolm (1989). "Werfel and Kafka." *Franz Werfel: An Austrian Writer Reassessed.* Ed. Lothar Huber. Oxford: Berg, 81–91.

Sandbank, Shimon (1989). "Comrade Kafka: Antifascist Fairy Tales of the Thirties." *After Kafka: The Influence of Kafka's Fiction.* Athens: University of Georgia Press.

Alter, Robert (1990). *Necessary Angels: Kafka, Benjamin, Scholem.* Cambridge: Harvard University Press.

Boa, Elizabeth (1990). "Feminist Approaches to Kafka's *Castle.*" *New Ways in Germanistik.* Ed. Richard Sheppard. New York and Oxford: Berg, 112–27.

Dowden, Stephen D. (1990). "Robinson Crusoe's Banner: Moral Imagination and Quixotic Nihilism in Franz Kafka's *The Castle.*" *Southern Humanities Review* 24:15–30.

Krippendorff, Ekkehart (1990). *Politische Interpretationen: Shakespeare, Stendhal, Balzac, Wagner, Hašek, Kafka, Kraus.* Frankfurt am Main: Suhrkamp.

Nägele, Rainer (1990). "Schloß ohne Schluß. Kafka, Benjamin und kein Ende." *Die Kunst zu enden.* Ed. Jürgen Söring. Frankfurt am Main: Suhrkamp, 163–186.

Neumann, Gerhard (1990). "Franz Kafkas Schloß-Roman. Das parasitäre Spiel der Zeichen." *Franz Kafka. Schriftverkehr.* Eds. Wolf Kittler and Gerhard Neumann. Freiburg: Rombach, 199–221.

Henry Sussman (1990). "The Circle of Exclusion: The Dissolution of Structure in Kafka's *Castle.*" *Afterimages of Modernity: Structure and Indifference in Twentieth-Century Literature.* Baltimore: Johns Hopkins University Press, 95–122.

Zilcosky, John (1990/91). "Kafka Approaches Schopenhauer's Castle." *German Life and Letters* 44:353–369.

Bloom, Allan (1991). "The Democritization of the University." *Giants and Dwarfs: Essays 1960–1990.* New York: Simon and Schuster, 365–87.

Cooper, Gabriele von Natzmer (1991). *Kafka and Language in the Stream of Thoughts and Life.* Riverside, California: Ariadne.

Jennings, Michael (1991). "'Eine gewaltige Erschütterung des Tradierten': Walter Benjamin's Political Recuperation of Kafka." Taubeneck 1991: 199–214.

Klingenstein, Susanne (1991). *Jews in the American Academy 1900–1940: The Dynamics of Intellectual Assimilation.* New Haven: Yale University Press.

Köppel, Peter (1991). *Die Agonie des Subjekts. Das Ende der Aufklärung bei Kafka und Blanchot.* Vienna: Passagen.

Kundera, Milan (1991). "In Saint Garda's Shadow: Rescuing Kafka from the Kafkologists." *Times Literary Supplement,* May 24, 3–5.

Lauter, Paul (1991). "University Reform: Threat or Opportunity?" *Canons and Contexts.* New York: Oxford University Press, 225–42.

Ryan, Judith (1991). "Franz Kafka." *The Vanishing Subject: Early Psychology and Literary Modernism.* Chicago and London: University of Chicago Press, 100–112.

Sokel, Walter H. (1991). "The Discovery of Austrian Literature under the Shadow of Nazism: Autobiography as a History of Reception of Literature." Taubeneck 1991:273–86.

Taubeneck, Steven, ed. (1991). *Fictions of Culture: Essays in Honor of Walter H. Sokel.* New York: Peter Lang.

Born, Jürgen (1992). "Kafka in America: His Growing Reputation during the Forties." *The Fortunes of German Writers in America: Studies in Literary Reception*. Eds. Wolfgang Elfe, James Hardin, Günther Holst. Columbia, S. C.: University of South Carolina Press.

Fischer, Dagmar (1992). *Kafkas "Schloß" Astralis. Eine "Divina Commedia" im "theatrum astronicum"*. 3 vols. Frankfurt am Main: Peter Lang.

Johnson, Uwe (1992). *Begleitumstände. Frankfurter Vorlesungen*. Frankfurt am Main: Suhrkamp.

Soderbergh, Steven (1992). *Kafka*. USA, England, France: Baltimore Pictures.

Alter, Robert (1993a). "Modernism and Nostalgia." *Partisan Review* 60:388–402.

Alter, Robert (1993b). "Kafka as Kabbalist." *Salmagundi* 98/99:86–99.

Blanchot, Maurice (1993). *Von Kafka zu Kafka*. Trans. Elsbeth Dangel. Frankfurt am Main: Fischer Taschenbuch, 1993.

Suchoff, David (1993). "Jüdische Kritiker in der amerikanischen Nachkriegsgermanistik." *Weimarer Beiträge* 39.3:393–409.

Walser, Martin (1993). *Des Lesers Selbstverständnis. Ein Bericht und eine Behauptung*. Parerga, 12. Eggingen: Edition Isele.

Heidsieck, Arnold (1994). *The Intellectual Contexts of Kafka's Fiction: Philosophy, Law, and Religion*. Columbia, S. C.: Camden House.

Linda C. Hsu (1994). "Klamotten: Reading Nietzsche Reading Kafka," *German Quarterly* 67.2:211–21.

Suchoff, David (1994). *Critical Theory and the Novel: Mass Society and Cultural Criticism in Dickens, Melville, and Kafka*. Madison: University of Wisconsin Press.

Index